Juba Arabic for Beginners

SIL International®

Editor-in-Chief

Mike Cahill

Managing Editor

Bonnie Brown

Volume Editor

Dirk Kievit

Production Staff

Lois Gourley, Composition Supervisor
Judy Benjamin, Compositor
Barbara Alber, Cover design

Cover Image

Juba Arabic for Beginners

Richard L. Watson

SIL International®
Dallas, TX

© 2015 by SIL International®
Library of Congress Catalog No: 2015941573
ISBN-978-1-55671-373-6

Printed in the United States of America

Copies of this and other publications of SIL International® may be obtained through distributors such as Amazon, Barnes & Noble, other worldwide distributors and, for select volumes, www.sil.org/resources/publications:

SIL International Publications
7500 W. Camp Wisdom Road
Dallas, TX 75236-5629 USA

General inquiry: publications_intl@sil.org
Pending order inquiry: sales_intl@sil.org
www.sil.org/resources/publications

Contents

Foreword

The citizens of South Sudan speak around sixty different languages, of which Juba Arabic is only one. Dr. Dick Watson of SIL, who wrote this book, was involved in training Sudanese teachers in a program of education in the mother tongue introduced by the Ministry of Education of the Southern Region of what was then Sudan in 1977. This program aimed to encourage more children to persevere with their schooling by making it easier for them to read and write, since they could learn in their mother tongues.

Once again, following the independence of South Sudan in 2011, it is possible to put a program of mother tongue education into effect. And once again, SIL is partnering in this vital endeavour by working with the Ministry of Education, Science, and Technology.

At the same time, the value of languages of wider communication should not be overlooked. Dick Watson wrote this course on Juba Arabic because he understood the importance of communication, and Juba Arabic is a form of Arabic used widely in South Sudan for communication between people who do not share a mother tongue. It binds together people of different ethnic backgrounds—even those with little or no education.

In reissuing this book, SIL–South Sudan hopes that many foreigners can be encouraged to learn a language which will bring them closer to ordinary South Sudanese and that at the same time they will come to appreciate the importance of language in any kind of development work.

Jackie Marshall
Director, SIL–South Sudan
Juba, South Sudan
February 2014

Abbreviations

The following abbreviations are used in this book:

adj	adjective
aux	auxiliary
conj	conjunction
ed.	educated Juba Arabic
lit.	literally
inter	interjection
n	noun
pass	passive
pl	plural
prep	preposition
pro	pronoun
sg	singular
trans	transitive verb
v	verb

1

Introduction to the course

This course is an adaptation of *Sudanese Colloquial Arabic for Beginners* by Andrew and Janet Persson with Ahmad Hussein, which was published by SIL in 1980. The original version of the Juba Arabic course was published in 1985. It has now been updated for South Sudan.

The purpose of the course is to help foreigners who have come to South Sudan talk with their South Sudanese colleagues, friends, and neighbors in the variety of Arabic spoken in Juba and most of the Equatoria Region. Students should notice differences in local dialects and adapt to them, as there are differences in pronunciation even within Juba between South Sudanese from different backgrounds. Students should therefore take guidance from the way their own teachers speak.

The lessons are designed to be used in either a class situation with a trained teacher or by individuals with a South Sudanese friend acting as "teacher." This course is not a reference grammar or a "teach yourself" book. The course has been written in Roman script for the benefit of students and teachers alike.

Each lesson contains a dialogue *("Kalaam")* and a vocabulary *("Kelimaat")* of new words introduced in the lesson. Most lessons also have a section with notes and drills *("Kelimaat Ziada al Der Arufu")* on new grammatical points as well as questions for practice *("Asilaat le Temriin")*. Following are some tips on getting the maximum benefit from each of these sections:

- **Dialogue:** First, students should listen as the teacher reads through the whole dialogue. After finishing, the teacher will read each phrase or full sentence separately; students should then repeat after

1

the instructor, taking care to imitate the pronunciation and intonation as closely as possible. Finally, the teacher should read through the entire dialogue once again. These dialogues should be memorized for thorough learning and use in practical situations.[1]

- **Vocabulary:** Students should memorize the vocabulary for each lesson. It is extremely difficult to make conversation unless students can recall basic vocabulary without conscious effort.

- **Notes and drills:** Students should read through the explanations and examples beforehand, then work through the drills with the teacher. Each drill should be performed in accordance with the instructions. For more practice, extra drills can be constructed resembling those in the lessons.

- **Questions for practice:** Students should practice the sample questions and answers, making up additional questions and answers as they practice. One of the keys to successful language learning is to "learn a little and use it a lot" (a phrase borrowed from Brewster and Brewster 1977:1). For this reason, it is important for students to learn to use their growing vocabulary in every situation as soon as possible and as often as possible.

No one should expect to learn to speak Juba Arabic simply by studying this course. As soon as students begin the first lesson, they must begin putting into practice what they have learned by speaking it with South Sudanese friends, shopkeepers, and anyone else they meet. South Sudanese are renowned for friendliness and hospitality, so no one needs to be afraid to try out the little Juba Arabic they know.

One of the best supplements to this course is carrying around a small notebook to write down new words and expressions you may hear. Students will also find it useful to record their teacher reading the dialogue and drills for each lesson so they can return to it later and practice on their own time. The book *Language Acquisition Made Practical (LAMP)* by Brewster and Brewster (see references) contains helpful instructions for recording procedures.

Although these lessons attempt to give a graduated development of vocabulary and grammatical constructions, students should not feel locked into the provided progression. Lessons or vignettes which students develop

---

[1]Since this course was first written in 1985, some of the dialogues may no longer be as current as they were originally. However, students will still benefit from studying these dialogues for the vocabulary and grammar. As opportunities arise, students can adapt these dialogues to their own situations.

in response to their own immediate needs and interests are more productive than those developed by anyone else. Students should therefore not hesitate to elicit words and texts on their own, make tape recordings for frequent listening, and ask the same questions of many people until they can predict their responses. Above all, it is important for students to spend time listening to the people and, as able, interacting with them. Also, students should not be afraid to jump ahead to a funeral or wedding lesson as the need arises—the other lessons will still be there to come back to. The key is for language learning to be relevant and enjoyable. Then, with perseverance, success is guaranteed.

For convenience, the vocabulary presented in the lessons is combined in the glossaries in the back of the book. Students may also wish to consult the newly released dictionary of Sudanese Arabic for additional vocabulary (also pubished by SIL; see references at the end of this course).

2

Pronunciation

This section gives an introduction to Juba Arabic pronunciation. Juba Arabic has omitted or changed several of the more difficult consonant sounds from Standard Arabic. In this regard it is considered a "simplified" language.

2.1 The consonant sounds

Following is a list of omitted or changed consonants:

Standard Arabic		"Educated" JA		Juba Arabic		Gloss
h	dahar	h or Ø	dahar/daar	Ø	daar	'back'
H	Humaar	h or Ø	humaar/umaar	Ø	umaar	'donkey'
gh	gharb	g	garb	g	garb	'west'
kh	khamsa	k	kamsa	k	kamsa	'five'
sh	shahar	sh or s	shaar/saar	s	saar	'month'
Z	ʕaawZ	z	auzu	j	auju	'want'
D	Dahar	d	daar	d	daar	'back'
S	Suura	s	sura	s	sura	'picture'
T	Talab	t	talab	t	talab	'order'
ʕ	ʕarabi	Ø	arabi	Ø	arabi	'Arabic'

In addition, double consonants in Standard Arabic[1] are replaced with single consonants in Juba Arabic. For example, *sukkar* 'sugar' and *da-khkhal* 'enter' are pronounced *sukar* and *dakalu* respectively in Juba Arabic.

"Educated" Juba Arabic varies, depending upon the speaker and the intended audience's experience in written Arabic or northern colloquial Arabic. With regard to pronunciation, the most noticeable characteristic is the use of *h* and *sh,* at least in some words. The *z* sound is a sign of education in some areas, but it is also common in some rural dialects where the vernacular uses it.

The full inventory of Juba Arabic consonants is given both in the chart below and in a listing with examples at the end of this section.

	bilabial	alveolar	alveo-palatal	velar	glottal
vl. plosive		t		k	(')
vd. plosive	b	d	j	g	
nasal	m	n	ny	ng	
vl. fricative	f	s	(sh)		(h)
vd. fricative	v	z			
lateral		l			
flap		r			
semi-vowel	w		y		

Voiced plosives (*b, d, j,* and *g*) are sometimes voiceless at the end of words and always voiceless at the end of utterances.

Glottal stops (') are rare but they are necessary in a few words, such as in *la'* meaning 'no'.

The voiceless fricative *f* not only involves the upper teeth and lower lip but also the upper lip. This can often be observed when a South Sudanese speaker pronounces the *f* in English words, as in *fill* or *fall.*

Alveopalatal *ny* occurs in a few words, such as *gony* 'frog'. Velar *ng* occurs in a few words, such as *neng.*

The *r* is flapped.

Though *sh* and *h* are rare in Juba Arabic, they are included in this course for the sake of those who want to use them. It is easier to drop them than it would be to add them if they were not written. However, *h* is not written at the end of words because it is never heard there in Juba Arabic, as in the word for South Sudanese pound, which is *jinee.*

---

[1]While genuine Arabic must be written in Arabic script, we apologize for the necessity of referring to a romanized form of standard Arabic.

2.2 The vowel sounds

The vowel sounds are basically *a, e, i, o,* and *u.* Each vowel may sound
either more close or more open, depending upon its environment. The
more open varieties occur in unstressed syllables, especially preceding
alveolar sounds, or in stressed syllables preceding *r.* For example, the *i*
of both syllables of *girish* 'piastre' is more open (like /i/ in English *it*)
than the *i* of *mile* 'salt'. The *e* of *deris* 'lesson' is more open (like /ɛ/ in
English *pen*) than the first *e* of *leben* 'milk'.

However, a word of caution is needed since English vowels are either
more close or more open than Arabic vowels. English close vowels are in
fact diphthongs; so, when a Juba Arabic vowel has diphthong quality, as
the *ei* in *kweis* 'good', English speakers pronounce it correctly; but, if not,
English speakers tend to shift all the way to an English open vowel. English
speakers must work at hitting "pure" vowels between the open and diphthong vowels of English. (Actually, if speakers can distinguish Advanced
Tongue Root vowels from Retracted Tongue Root vowels, they may come
even closer to the real vowels of Juba Arabic.)

There are two uses for double vowels in Juba Arabic spelling. First, two identical vowels occur together in words where the Standard Arabic *h, H,* or ʕ have
been omitted, as in *saar* for *shahar* 'month', *teet* for *tiHit* 'under', or *saa* for *saʕa*
'hour'. Double vowels in these cases are considered to belong to separate syllables and require double pronunciation, e.g., /sa.ar/ or /sa.id/ 'help'. However,
note that some speakers simplify double vowels to single, e.g., /sar/, /tet/, /sa/.
(In this course, *h* is usually written for Standard Arabic *h* and *H,* even though it
is only pronounced by educated speakers, but ʕ is never written.)

Additionally, double vowels are used to indicate the stressed syllable of
a word when it is not the first syllable, e.g., *umbaari* /um.'ba.ri/. This can
sometimes lead to a situation with three identical vowels in a row. For
example, the word /ta.'al/ 'come' is stressed on the second syllable, so the
second-syllable vowel is doubled. This would therefore be written as *taaal.*
To avoid three *a*'s in a row, a hyphen is inserted between the two syllables,
i.e., *ta-aal.* When the vowels are not alike, the hyphen is not needed, e.g.,
boiid 'far' or *yauu* 'this here'.

2.3 Word stress and syllable structures

Most words are stressed on the first syllable; however, stress is not pre-
dictable. A stressed vowel is not long but combines force and high pitch.
As stated in the previous section, double vowels are written to indicate
stress when it is not on the first syllable. Double vowels are used because
diacritics such as an apostrophe (') are messy and easily omitted; and because stressed syllables, other than first syllables, usually correspond to

long vowels in Standard Arabic. For example, *katiir* 'much' in Standard Arabic is stressed on the second syllable because the vowel is long. In Juba Arabic most words are stressed on the same syllable as in Standard Arabic, but not because of vowel length, as there is no vowel length in Juba Arabic. For this reason it is not necessary to write one-syllable words as long, e.g., *bet* 'house', though it is *beet* in Standard Arabic.

Word stress is sometimes grammatical. For example, *weledu* (stressed on the first syllable) is an active verb, meaning 'to give birth', but *weleduu* (stressed on the final syllable) is a passive verb, meaning 'to be born'.

There are a few diphthongs, written with *y* or *w,* e.g., *aynu* 'look!', which contrasts with *ainu* 'see, look'. However, most adjacent vowels are not diphthongs, e.g., /a.i.nu/ is three syllables.

2.4 Examples of consonants and vowels

The list of examples below is given for students to become somewhat familiar with all of the consonant and vowel sounds before starting lesson one. The teacher should read through each group of words for the students to listen; then, the teacher should read each word for the students to mimic. It is not necessary to master each sound before going on to lesson one.

Caution: the teacher must understand that these words are not to be learned as vocabulary items but only to be practiced for pronunciation. English meanings are given only to ensure that the Juba Arabic word practiced is the one intended.

Consonants

b	bab	'door'		kamaan	'and, also'
	bed gidaad	'chicken egg'		kamsa	'five'
	bedri	'early'		kalaas	'finished'
d	degiig	'flour'		kokoora	'redivision'
	deris	'lesson'	l	leben	'milk'
	dakulu	'enter'		lemuun	'lemon'
	dahar	'back'		lisa	'not yet'
f	fatuur	'breakfast'	m	moya	'water'
	afamu	'understand'		medereesa	'school'
	fil	'elephant'		mumkin	'possible'
g	guruush	'money'	n	nas	'people'
	gufa	'basket'		aniina	'we'
	ganamooya	'goat'		num	'sleep'
	garb	'west'		nahaar de	'today'
h	hawa	'air'	r	rajil	'man'

	habuub	'wind, storm'		rakabu	'cook'
	helu	'sweet'		rotaan	'language'
	humaar	'donkey'	s	samaga	'fish'
j	jibu	'give, bring'		suk	'market'
	jawaab	'letter'		sa	'hour, watch'
	jebel	'hill'		sabuun	'soap'
k	ketiir	'many'		senduuk	'box'
	kubri	'bridge'		sura	'picture'
sh/s	shamaal	'north'	w	waid/wahid	'one'
	ashurubu	'drink'		wenu	'where'
	shubaak	'window'		welid	'boy'
t	tani	'again'	y	yamiin	'right'
	talaata	'three'		yom	'day'
	teksi	'taxi'		yauu de	'here'
	tawaali	'straight'	z	zol	'person'
	talab	'order, request'		zerif	'envelope'
	tilmiis	'pupil, student'		zahare	'purple'

Vowels

	Bari	'Bari people'		min	'from'
a	haja	'thing'		kis	'bag'
	mara	'woman'		ketiir	'much'
	talaata	'three'		gebiila	'tribe'
aa*	laam/laham	'meat'	o	gowi	'hard'
	baar/bahar	'river'		kokoora	'redivision'
	ta-aal	'come'		zol	'person'
e	geni	'live'		yom	'day'
	bileel	'night'		okot	'sister'
	bet	'house'	u	sukar	'sugar'
	esh	'bread'		mumkin	'possible'
ee**	teet/tehet	'under'		ainu	'see'
i	ita	'you'		sabuun	'soap'
	mile	'salt'		lemuun	'lemon'

*when *h* or ʕ is dropped
**when *h* is dropped

Deris nimira wahid
Fi dukaan

Lesson 1
At the shop

Kalaam maa sidu dukaan
(Z: zabuun, S: sidu dikaan)

'Dialogue with a shopkeeper'
(Z: 'customer', S: 'shopkeeper')

Z: Salaam taki. — 'Hello.'
S: Ahlen. — 'Welcome.'
Z: Ita kweis? — 'Are you well?'
S: Ana kweis, ma bataal. Ita kweis? — 'I am well, not bad. Are you well?'
Z: Kweis, ya sabii. Sabuun kasiil fi le ita? — 'Good. Do you have washing soap?'
S: Ai fi. Ita deru kam? — 'Yes, I have. How much do you want?'
Z: Jibu le ana itiniin. Fi sukar? — 'Give me two. Is there sugar?'
S: Sukar kalasu. — 'The sugar is all gone.'
Z: De shunuu? — 'What is this?'
S: De mile. Ita deru mile? — 'This is salt. Do you want salt?'
Z: Ai, kis to be kam? — 'Yes, how much is a bag of it?'
S: Kis to be itniin jinee. — 'A bag of it is two pounds.'
Z: Jibu le ana wahid. — 'Give me one.'
S: Ita deru haja tani? — 'Do you want anything else?'
Z: Kalaas, ana ma deru haja tani. Shukran. — 'That's all. I don't want anything else. Thank you.'
S: Kalaas, shukran. Maa salaam taki. — 'That's all, thank you. Goodbye.'

Kelimaat ziada al der arufu

'Extra things you want to know'

1. The *u* between *sid* 'owner, keeper' and *dukaan* 'shop' is a transitional vowel, used to separate two consonants, especially in the case of two *d*'s. Likewise, *i* separates *t* and *n* in *itiniin* 'two'.

2. In greetings, singular and plural forms are distinguished, but there are
    no masculine-feminine distinctions.

    a. Both *salaam taki* and *salamaat* are singular forms for 'hello'; *sa-
        laam takum* and *salamaatkum* are plural forms. (Some people say
        that *salamaatkum* is used only when a person has narrowly avoided
        death, though not all agree with this interpretation.)

    b. The reply is usually *ahlen* 'welcome' or *salaam taki kamaan* 'your
        peace also'.

    c. *Kweis* 'good/well/okay' is singular; *kweisiin* is plural.

3. Personal pronouns also distinguish singular-plural but not masculine-
    feminine. For the following list, repeat each example after the teacher.
    Then, respond with the appropriate phrase as the teacher indicates
    which person(s).

Ana kweis.	'I'm well.'
Aniina kweisiin.	'We are well.'
Ita kweis.	'You are well.'
Itakum kweisiin.	'You *(pl)* are well.'
Huwo kweis.	'He/she is well.'
Humon kweisiin.	'They are well.'

    Next, use the same phrases for questions and answers. For example:

Ita kweis?	'Are you well?'
Ai, ana kweis.	'Yes, I'm well.'

4. Possessive pronouns follow the thing possessed; e.g., *kis taki* 'your bag'
    kis to 'his/her/its bag'.

5. Statements and yes-no questions differ only in intonation. *De mile* 'This
    is salt' has falling tone on the last syllable, but *De mile?* 'Is this salt?'
    has rising tone on the last syllable. Content questions—e.g., *De shunuu?*
    'What is this?'—have a falling tone, like statements.

    Repeat each example after the teacher. Then, respond with an appropri-
    ate phrase when the teacher points to a picture.

De mile.	'This is salt.'
De esh.	'This is bread.'

De zet.	'This is oil.'
De shay.	'This is tea.'
De sukar.	'This is sugar.'
De bed gidaada.	'This is an egg.'
De degiig.	'This is flour.'
De laham.	'This is meat.'
De sabuun.	'This is soap.'
De kis.	'This is a bag.'
De shunuu?	'What is this?'

Next, make and respond to yes-no questions. For example:

De mile?	'Is this salt?'
Ai, de mile. Ita deru mile?	'Yes, this is salt. Do you want salt?'
La', de ma mile, de esh.	'No, this isn't salt, it's bread.'

6. The verb *fi* 'exist' means 'there is/are' or 'have/possess'. For example:

Fi mile?	'Is there salt?'
Ai, fi mile.	'Yes, there is salt.'
La', mafi mile.	'No, there is no salt.'
Fi le ita mile?	'Do you have any salt?'
Ai, fi le ana mile.	'Yes, I have salt.'
La', mafi le ana mile.	'No, I don't have any salt.'

Practice these phrases as the teacher points to various persons and pictures of food items. (It is also correct to say *Fi mile le ita?* or *Mile fi le ita?*)

7. *Deru* 'want', like all verbs in Juba Arabic, does not distinguish person or gender; however, it is an exception as it sometimes distinguishes singular and plural. The plural form *deriin* is used in these lessons, but it is common to hear *deru* for plural as well. Repeat the following phrases after the teacher. Then, respond with the appropriate phrase as the teacher points.

Ita deru laham?	'Do you want meat?'
Ai, ana deru laham.	'Yes, I want meat.'
La', ana ma deru laham.	'No, I don't want meat.'
Huwo deru esh?	'Does he/she want bread?'
Ai, huwo deru esh.	'Yes, he/she wants bread.'
La', huwo ma deru esh.	'No he/she does not want bread.'
Itakum deriin sukar?	'Do you want sugar?'
Ai, aniina deriin sukar.	'Yes, we want sugar.'
La', aniina ma deriin sukar.	'No, we don't want sugar.'

Humon deriin sabuun?	'Do they want soap?'
Ai, humon deriin sabuun.	'Yes, they want soap.'
La', humon ma deriin sabuun.	'No, they don't want soap.'

Auzu or *auju* 'want' is also quite common, though not used in these lessons. *Azu* or *aju* is heard in some dialects.

8. *Jibu* means 'bring', but it is also used for 'give/hand me'. Practice this verb with various pronouns and objects as the teacher points. For example:

Jibu le ana sukar.	'Give me sugar.'
Jibu le huwo sukar.	'Give him sugar.'
Jibu aniina sukar.	'Give us sugar.'
Jibu le humon sukar.	'Give them sugar.'

9. *Be* is a preposition meaning 'by, for', e.g., *be kam?* 'for how much?' or *be arba jinee* 'for four pounds'.

Notice that every English clause must contain a verb, but a Juba Arabic equative clause does not contain a verb, e.g., *kis to be kam?* 'bag of-it for-how-much?' i.e., 'How much does a bag of it cost?'.

Practice asking the prices of various items and answering with *wahid jinee* 'one pound', *itiniin jinee* 'two pounds', or *arba jinee* 'four pounds'. Don't try to give realistic prices since these are the only numbers you have studied at present.

Esh be kam?	'How much is bread?'
Esh be arba jinee.	'Four pounds.'
Mile be kam?	'How much is salt?'
Mile be itiniin jinee.	'Two pounds.'

10. The simple form of most verbs ends in *-u,* which could be called a verb-marking suffix. This simple form is past tense unless it is used as an imperative, e.g., *jibu* 'bring, give!'. The glosses should give the *-ed* 'past' form of the English. However, for simplicity we usually use only the simple form of the English (which is either imperative or present tense).

11. The main staples in South Sudan, not mentioned in the lesson, are *dura* 'millet, sorghum' and *isheriif* 'maize/corn'. *Ruz* 'rice' is also available, but *game'* 'wheat' is not, except as flour.

Kelimaat 'Vocabulary'

ahlen	'welcome' *(greeting)*
ai	'yes'
ana	'I/me'
aniina	'we/us'
arba	'four'
arufu/arifu	'know'
auzu	'want, need'; cf. *deru*
bataal	'bad'
be/bi	'by, for'
bed gidaada	'chicken egg'
bitaaki/taki	'your(s), of you *(sg)*'
bitaakum/takum	'your(s), of you *(pl)*'
de	'this'
degiig	'flour'
deriin	'want *(pl)*'
deris (*pl* derisiaat)	'lesson'
deru	'want, need'; cf. *auzu*
dukaan (*pl* dukanaat)	'shop, store'
dura	'millet, sorghum, grain'
esh	'bread'
fi	'there is/are, have, possess, exist'
game'	'wheat'
guruush	'money'
haja (*pl* hajaat)	'thing'
humon	'they/them'
huwo	'he/him, she/her, it'
isheriif	'maize, corn'
ita	'you *(sg)*'
itakum	'you *(pl)*'
itiniin/itniin	'two'
jibu	'bring, hand, give'
jinee	'pound (SSP=South Sudanese Pound)'
kalaam	'talk, dialogue'
kalaas	'finished, okay' *(adj)*
kalasu	'finish, finished'
kam	'how much, many'
kamaan	'also'
kasiil	'clothes-washing'
kelima (*pl* kelimaat)	'word'
kis (*pl* kisiaat)	'bag'

kweis(a)/kwesii (*pl* kweisiin)	'good, well, okay'
la'	'no'
laham/laam	'meat'
le	'to'
ma	'not'
maa/ma	'with'
maa salaam taki/takum	'goodbye (lit. with your peace *sg/pl*)'
mile	'salt'
nimira (*pl* nimiraat)	'number'
ruz	'rice'
sabuun	'soap'
salaam	'hello (lit. peace)'
salaam taki	'hello (lit. peace to you, *sg*)'
salaam takum	'hello (lit. peace to you, *pl*)'
salamaat	'hello *(sg)*'
salamaatkum	'hello *(pl)*'
shay	'tea'
shukran/sukuran	'thank you'
shunuu	'what?'
sid	'owner, keeper'
sukur	'sugar'
taki/bitaaki	'your(s), of you *(sg)*'
takum/bitaakum	'your(s), of you *(pl)*'
tani	'else, other'
to/tou	'his/of him; hers/of her; its/of it'
wahid/waid	'one'
zabuun (*pl* zabunaat)	'customer'
zet	'oil'
ziada	'more'

Deris nimira itiniin
Fi suk

Lesson 2
At the market

Kalaam fi suk
(K: Kamiisa, S: sid, T: Tereesa)

'Dialogue in the market'
(K: Kamiisa, S: 'owner', T: Teresa)

K: Ana deru laham, ya rajil. Kilo be kam?

'I want some meat, man. How much is a kilo?'

S: Kilo be ashara jinee. Ita deru kam kilo?

'A kilo is ten pounds. How many kilos do you want?'

(Humon ruwa fi mahaal samaga.)

('They go to the fish place.')

T: Ana deru samaga. De be kam?

'I want some fish. How much is this piece?'

S: De be tisa jinee.

'This one is nine pounds.'

T: De ketiir kalis. Nagisu shweya.

'That's too much. Reduce it a little.'

S: Kweis, jibu saba jinee.

'Okay, give me seven pounds.'

(Humon ruwa fi mahaal fawaaki.)

('They go to the fruit place.')

K: Ya John, aniina deriin talaata bed gidaada u wahid kom ta lemuun u wahid kom ta manga u wahid kom ta bataatis. Kulu be kam?

'John, we want three chicken eggs, one pile of lemons, one pile of mangos and one pile of potatoes. How much for all of that?'

S: Kulu be tamaanya jinee.

'All of that comes to eight pounds.'

K: De ketiir. Nagisu shweya—aniina zabuun taki.

'That's a lot. Reduce it a little—we are your customers.'

S: Kweis, ashaan itakum zabuun bitaai, jibu takum saba jinee.

'Okay, because you are my customer, give me seven pounds.'

17

K: Shukran, ya John. Jibu kulu fi gufa   'Thank you, John. Bring it all to
   de.   this basket.'

Kelimaat ziada al der arufu

1. *Fi* in lesson 1 was the verb 'exist', but in this lesson it is a preposition
   meaning 'in/at'. It can also be used where we would expect *le* 'to', e.g.,
   ruwa fi bet 'went home'.

Practice the following drill by substituting all of the pronouns and names
into the subject position and all of the locations into the locative position.

Ana ruwa fi suk.   'I went to the market.'
Aniina ruwa fi mahaal laham.   'We went to the meat place.'
Huwo ruwa fi mahaal samaga.   'He went to the fish place.'
Kamiisa ruwa fi mahaal fawaaki.   'Kamisa went to the fruit place.'
Tereesa ruwa fi dukaan.   'Teresa went to the shop.'

2. You may have already noticed in the drill above that the word for 'go/
   went' may sound like either *ruwa* or *rowa*. Imitate your teacher. You
   may also hear either *masi* or *mashi* for 'go'.

3. *Ya* is a vocative particle which is always used in addressing a person,
   regardless of whether one uses the person's name, a pronoun, or any
   other designation. For example:

ya John   'John'
ya ita   'you'
ya weled   'boy'

4. *Yauu de* 'here is' is used in handing something or in pointing to something close at hand. Practice using *yauu de* as you hand things or point
   to things:

Yauu de guruush taki.   'Here is your money.'
Yauu de lemuun taki.   'Here is your lemon.'
Yauu de bataatis taki.   'Here is your potato.'

Notice that some nouns are collective nouns which can be either singular
or plural without changing form. For example, the last two sentences could
as well be translated as 'here are your lemons' and 'here are your potatoes'.

5. Bargaining over prices is cultural; however, it is best to learn prices before beginning to bargain. Some prices are fixed very low and cannot

be lowered. Some salesmen only make a small mark-up and could not afford to cut the price very much while others will try to take advantage of a foreigner and can afford a large reduction. Another useful phrase in bargaining is *Fi le ana...* 'I have...', meaning '...is all I am willing to pay'.

6. *U* 'and' is used to separate all items in a series, not just the last item as in English, e.g., *lemuun u bataatis u laham u degiig* 'lemons and potatoes and meat and flour'. *Wa* is another form of 'and'.

7. You have now learned four of the six possessive pronouns and the other two are easy to learn. Practice them with any nouns.

De zabuun tai.	'This is my customer.'
De dukaan taki.	'This is your shop.'
De fawaaki to.	'This is his fruit.'
De bataatis taniina.	'These are our potatoes.'
De lemuun takum.	'These are your lemons.'
De laham tomon.	'This is their meat.'

8. Imperatives are formed by the simple verb. *Takum* 'your' is added to make the plural. Practice making imperatives like the following:

jibu	'bring, give me'
jibu takum	'bring, give me (you all)'
ruwa	'go'
ruwa takum	'go (you all)'
nagisu	'reduce'
nagisu takum	'reduce (you all)'

9. You have now covered numbers 1–10, except for *sita* 'six'. Practice counting as the teacher holds up one or more fingers and names objects. For example:

wahid rajil	'one man'
wahid deris	'one lesson'
wahid jinee	'one pound'
itiniin lemuun	'two lemons'
talaata lemuun	'three lemons'
araba lemuun	'four lemons'
kamsa lemuun	'five lemons'
sita kom	'six piles'
sita kilo	'six kilos'
sita jinee	'six pounds'
saba bataatis	'seven potatoes'

tamaanya bataatis	'eight potatoes'
tisa bataatis	'nine potatoes'
ashara bataatis	'ten potatoes'

Note: singular nouns can be used in the plural sense (see lesson 6).

11. Prices are stated in whole pounds. There are no coins. Some of the prices in this lesson may not be entirely realistic since numbers above ten are not taught till a later lesson.

12. Ordinal numbers use the word *nimira* 'number', e.g., *deris nimira wahid* 'the first lesson'.

13. The prefix *bi-* often occurs with *ta* 'of' or with a possessive pronoun, e.g., *bitaa Tereesa* 'of Teresa' or *bitoo* 'his/hers'. The forms *ta* and *bitaa* are almost interchangeable; however, *bitaa* tends to be used more as a predicate, e.g., *De bitaa Tereesa* 'This belongs to Teresa'. The possessive forms with and without the prefix are as follows:

bitaai/tai	'of me, my, mine'
bitaaki/taki	'of you, your(s) *(sg)*'
bitoo(u)/to(u)	'of it/its; of him, his; of her/her(s)'
bitaniina/taniina	'of us, our(s)'
bitaakum/takum	'of you, your(s) *(pl)*'
bitoomon/tomon	of them, their(s)'

Kelimaat

ashaan	'because'
ashara	'ten'
asila (*pl* asilaat)	'question'
asma(u)/asuma	'hear, listen, obey'
bataatis	'potato(es)'
bitaa/ta	'of, belong to'
bitaai/tai	'of me, my, mine'
bitaniina/taniina	'of us, our(s)'
bitoo(u)/to(u)	'of him/her/it; his/her(s)/its'
bitoomon/tomon	'of them, their(s)'
dasta	'dozen'
fawaaki	'fruit'
fi	'in, at, to'
ful	'peanuts, groundnuts'
gufa (*pl* gufaat)	'basket'

kalis	'very'
kamsa/kamiisa	'five'
ketiir	'(too) much/many'
kilo	'kilo'
kom	'pile'
koroofo	'greens'
kulu	'all, every'
lemuun	'lemon(s)'
maal (*pl* malaat)/	'place'
mahaal (*pl* mahalaat)	
manga	'mango(es)'
masi/mashi	'go/went'
nagisu	'reduce, discount'
nus	'half'
rajil (*pl* rujaliin)	'man'
ruwa/rowa	'go, went'
saba	'seven'
samaga	'fish'
shweya	'a little'
sita	'six'
suk (*pl* sukaat)	'market'
ta/bitaa	'of, belong to'
tai/bitaai	'my, of me'
talaata/telaata	'three'
tamaanya	'eight'
taniina/bitaniina	'of us, our(s)'
temriin	'drills'
tisa	'nine'
to(u)/bitoo(u)	'of him/her/it; his/her(s)/its'
tomon/bitoomon	'of them, their(s)'
u/wa	'and'
weled/welid/woled (*pl* awlaad)	'boy, son, child'
ya	vocative
yauu de	'here is'

Asilaat le temriin 'Questions for practice'

1. Sidu dukaan fi mile le huwo?   Ai, fi mile le huwo.
2. Sidu dukaan fi sukar le huwo?   La', sukar kalasu.
3. Sidu dukaan fi laham le huwo?   Ai, sidu dukaan fi laham le huwo.
4. Tereesa deru laham?   La', Kamiisa deru laham.
5. Tereesa deru shunuu?   Tereesa deru samaga.
6. Kilo ta laham be kam?   Kilo be ashara jinee.

7. Samaga be kam?   Samaga be tisa jinee.
8. Sidu samaga nagisu shweya?   Ai, huwo nagisu shweya.
9. Sidu dukaan nagisu shweya?   La', sidu dukaan ma nagisu.
10. Kamiisa deru dasta ta shunuu?   Kamiisa deru dasta ta bed gidaada.
11. Kamiisa deru dasta ta degiig?   La', huwo deru kilo ta degiig.
12. Fi kam manga fi kom?   Fi ____ manga fi kom.
13. Fi kam bataatis fi kom?   Fi ____ bataatis fi kom.
14. Kilo bataatis be kam?   Kilo bataatis be ____.
15. Fi zabuun le John?   Ai, Kamiisa u Tereesa zabuun bitoo.
16. Fi suk fi talaata mahalaat?   Ai, fi.
17. Fi mahalaat shunuu fi suk?   Fi suk fi mahaal laham u mahaal
                                         samaga u mahaal fawaaki.
18. Fi suk fi mahaal tani?   Ai, fi mahalaat ketiir.
19. Fi kam nimiraat fi deris nimira 1?   Fi talaata nimiraat: wahid u itiniin u
                                         arba.
20. Fi kam nimiraat tani fi deris   Fi saba nimiraat tani: talaata u
    nimira 2?   kamsa u sita u saba u tamaanya u
                                         tisa u ashara.
21. Ita deru ruwa fi suk?   Ai, ana deru.
                                         La', ana ma deru.

Deris nimira talaata
Ma zol ja ainu bet

Lesson 3
With a visitor

Kalaam ma zol ja ainu bet
(Z: zol ja ainu bet, R: rajil, M: mara)

'Dialogue with a visitor'
(Z: 'visitor', R: 'man', M: 'woman')

Z: Salamaat.

R: Ahlen, salaam taki.

Z: Ita kweis?

R: Ana kweis, taal geni.

Z: Ita derisu Arabi de min wen?

R: Ana derisu Arabi de fi Juba. Fadal, ashrubu moya.

Z: Ita alimu Arabi de kweis.
   (Mara dakulu.)

M: Salamaatkum.

Z: Salaam taki, ya mara. Ita kweis?

R: Jibu lemuun u amulu le aniina bun. (le zol) Ita akulu fatuur?

Z: Lisa.

R: Ana ashrubu bun gibeel, lakiin ana ma akulu fatuur. Ashrubu lemuun. Fatuur amuluu kalaas.

Z: Itakum derisu Arabi de fi medereesa wala itakum derisu fi bet?

'Hello.'

'Welcome. Hello.'

'Are you well?'

'I'm fine, come in and sit down.'

'Where did you study this Arabic?'

'I studied this Arabic in Juba. Please drink some water.'

'You learned this Arabic well.'
('Woman enters.')

'Hello.'

'Hello, madam. Are you well?'

'Bring lemonade and make coffee. (to visitor) Have you eaten breakfast?'

'Not yet.'

'I drank coffee already, but I haven't eaten breakfast. Drink some lemonade. Breakfast is made.'

'Did you *(pl)* study Arabic at school or at home?'

23

R: Aniina derisu Arabi de fi bet, badi dak aniina derisu fi medreesa le muda talaata shuhuur.

'We studied this Arabic at home, after that we studied at school for a period of three months.'

Z: Fatuur kweis, shukran.

'Breakfast was good, thank you.'

R: Afwan.

'You are welcome.'

Kelimaat ziada al der arufu

1. The word *defaan* 'visitor' is known, but the phrase *zol ja ainu bet* 'person who comes to see the house' is more common.

2. *Arabi de* 'this Arabic' refers to 'this dialect of Arabic'.

3. *Fadal* is an invitation to proceed an action, e.g., 'come in/sit down/eat/drink'. The specific invitation is often stated together with it, e.g., *fadal, ashrubu moya* 'go ahead and drink water'.

4. The adverb *wen* 'where' may be used with or without a preposition, as explained below:

   a. It may be used *with* a preposition, such as *min* 'from', as in this lesson: *Ita derisu Arabi de min wen?* 'Where did you study Arabic from?' Compare also *Ita ja min wen?* 'Where did you come from?' and *Ita jibu laham min wen?* 'Where did you bring meat from?'

   b. It may also be used *without* a preposition, as in *Ita ruwa wen* 'Where did you go?' Other examples:

Ita akulu fatuur wen?	'Where did you eat breakfast?'
Ita ashrubu moya wen?	'Where did you drink water?'
Ita ainu huwo wen?	'Where did you see him?'

   c. *Wenu* 'where' adds *u,* and functions as a verb, when no other verb is present.

Ita wenu?	Ana (fi) fi bet.	'I am at home.'
Huwo wenu?	Huwo____medereesa.	'He is at school.'
Esh wenu?	Esh____dukaan.	'Bread is at the store.'
Manga wenu?	Manga____mahaal fawaaki.	'Mangos are at the fruit place.'
Mara wenu?	Mara____suk.	'The woman is at the market.'
Zol wenu?	Zol____bet.	'The person is at the house.'
Lemuun wenu?	Lemuun____mahaal fawaaki.	'Lemons are at the fruit place.'

Samaga wenu? Samaga_____mahaal   'Fish is at the fish place.'
                     samaga.

(The verb *fi* 'be' is optional, whereas the preposition *fi* 'in/at' is not.) *Wenu* can also precede the noun, e.g., *Wenu esh?* 'Where is bread?' However, it cannot precede a pronoun or a proper noun, i.e., *Ita wenu?* and *John wenu?* should not be reversed.

5.   In a passive construction, the subject is the logical object (thing affected) and the final vowel of the verb is stressed (written by doubling the *u*), as in *fatuur amuluu* 'breakfast is made'. Other examples:

moya ashrubuu	'the water is drunk'
lemuun ashrubuu	'the lemonade is drunk'
fatuur akuluu	'breakfast is eaten'
deris derisuu	'the lesson is studied'
guruush jibuu	'the money is brought'
samaga nagisuu	'the fish is reduced'
sukar kalasuu	'the sugar is finished'
gada akuluu	'lunch is eaten'
asha akuluu	'supper is eaten'
fatuur amuluu kalaas	'breakfast is made'
bun amuluu kalaas	'the coffee is made'
mile kalasuu	'the salt is finished'
bun kalasuu	'the coffee is finished'

Note: the last verb, *kalasuu,* can be passive without changing stress, e.g., *sukar kalasu.*

6.   Practice the following sentences with adverbs and adverbial phrases:

Ana deresu ketiir.	'I studied much.'
Ana ashrubu bun gibeel.	'I drank coffee already.'
Ita deresu Arabi kweis.	'You studied Arabic well.'
Huwo alimu Arabi kweis.	'He learned Arabic well.'
John nagisu samaga shweya.	'John reduced the fish a little.'
Aniina amalu kalaas.	'We finished making it.'
Aniina deresu Arabi le muda talaata shuhuur.	'We studied Arabic for a period of three months.'

7.   In this lesson, sentences are compounded by the use of *lakiin* 'but' and *badi dak* 'after that'.

   a.   Practice contrasts with *lakiin* 'but':

Ana ashrubu shay lakiin ma ashrubu bun.	'I drank tea but not coffee.'
Ana ashrubu moya lakiin ma ashrubu lemuun.	'I drank water but not lemonade.'
Ana akulu fatuur lakiin ma aku-lu gada.	'I ate breakfast but not dinner.'
Ana akulu manga lakiin ma aku-lu laham.	'I ate mango but not meat.'
Ana ruwa fi suk lakiin ma ruwa fi mahaal samaga.	'I went to the market but not to the fish place.'
Ana derisu Arabi lakiin ma al-imu kweis.	'I studied Arabic but didn't learn well.'
Fi le ana wahid manga lakiin mafi le ana itiniin manga.	'I have one mango but not two mangos.'
Huwo zabuun lakiin ana ma zabuun.	'He is a customer but I'm not.'
Huwo sidu dukaan lakiin ana zabuun to.	'He is a shopkeeper but I'm his customer.'

b. Practice the following sequences with *badi dak* 'after that':

Huwo ruwa fi medereesa, badi dak huwo ruwa fi suk.	'He went to school, after that he went to the market.'
Huwo ashrubu bun, badi dak huwo ashrubu moya.	'He drank coffee, after that he drank water.'
Huwo jibu laham, badi dak huwo jibu bataatis.	'He brought meat, after that he brought potatoes.'

8. *Ainu* 'see, look' is used in these lessons, though *shufu* 'see, look' is also common.

Ita ainu bet taniina?	'Have you seen our house?'
Ana deru ita ja ainu.	'I want you to come see it.'
Ita ainu medereesa tai?	'Have you seen my school?'
Ana deru ita ja ainu.	'I want you to come see it.'
Ainu zol dak.	'Look at that person.'
Ainu moya de.	'Look at this water.'

Kelimaat

afwan	'you're welcome'
ainu	'see, look'; cf. shufu
akulu	'eat/ate'
alimu	'understand, learn'

amulu/amalu	'make, do'
amuluu	'was made'
Arabi	'Arabic'
asha	'supper'
ashrubu/ashribu	'drink'
badi	'after'
bet (*pl* biyuut)	'house, home'
bun	'coffee'
dak	'that'
dakulu	'enter'
defaan (*pl* defanaat)	'guest, visitor'
derisu/deresu	'study'
fadal	'please' (invitation)
fatuur	'breakfast'
gada	'dinner'
geni	'sit down'
gibeel	'already'
ja	'come, came'
lakiin	'but'
lemuun	'lemonade'
lisa	'still, not yet'
mara (*pl* mariaat, niswaan)	'woman, wife'
medereesa	'school'
min	'from'
moya	'water'
moya lemuun	'lemonade'
muda	'period of time'
shahar/saar (*pl* shuhuur)	'month'
shufu	'see, look'; cf. ainu
taal	'come!'
wala	'or'
wen/wenu	'where'
zol (*pl* nas)	'person'

Deris nimira arba
Fi bab

Lesson 4
At the gate

Kalaam fi bab
(R: rajil, W: welid, K: kadaam)

'Dialogue at the gate'
(R: 'man', W: 'boy', K: 'house worker')

R: Ita, ya welid, James gi geni ini?
W: Ai, bet tomon geriib ma dukaan.
R: Shukran.
   (Huwo gi dugu bab u kadaam gi
   fata bab.)
R: James fi?
K: La', huwo safiru umbaari.
R: Huwo safiru le wen?
K: Huwo ma mara to safiru le Yei.
R: Humon arkabu bas wala lori?
K: Humon arkabu bas.
R: Fi zol tomon ayaan fi Yei?
K: La', wahid min akwaana tomon
   rija min bara.
R: Yal to fi fi bet?
K: La', humon rowa hasi de.
R: Mata fekiru. Sa kam?
K: Sa kamsa.

'Hey boy, does James live here?'
'Yes, their house is near the shop.'
'Thank you.'
('He knocks on the door and a
house worker opens it.')
'Is James in?'
'No, he traveled yesterday.'
'Where did he travel?'
'He and his wife traveled to Yei.'
'Did they ride the bus or lorry?'
'They rode the bus.'
'Is one of their people sick in Yei?'
'No, one of their brothers returned
from abroad.'
'Are his children at home?'
'No, they just left.'
'Never mind. What time is it?'
'Five o'clock.'

R: Shukran, ma salaam taki.
K: Ma salaam taki kamaan.

'Thank you. Goodbye.'
'Goodbye also.'

29

Kelimaat ziada al der arufu

1. Progressive aspect is marked by *gi* or *ge*. Throughout this course, *gi* is
    used, but *ge* is considered by some to be more accurate as it is derived
    from *geni* 'stay, sit'. In application, some join it to the verb. Practice the
    following substitution drill:

James gi geni.	'James is sitting, staying.'
Huwo ___ ruwa.	'He is going.'
Ana ___ dugu.	'I am hitting.'
Ita ___ fata.	'You are opening.'
John ___ safiru.	'John is traveling.'
John ___ arkabu	'John is riding'
John ___ ja	'John is coming'
John ___ fekiru	'John is think'
John ___ derisu	'John is study'

2. Most verbs add a lightly pronounced *u*. However, some verbs ending
    in vowels never add *u*, and some verbs ending in a consonant or vowel
    sometimes add *u*. Following are examples of these three groupings.
    (Some dialects use the suffix -*u* less than others and it is often dropped
    from imperatives.) The *u* is especially light following *b* or *m*, e.g., *ashra-
    bu, kelimu*.
    > Always add *u*: *derisu* 'study', *akulu* 'eat', *ashrubu* 'drink'
    > Never add *u*: *ruwa* 'go', *ja* 'come', *rija* 'return', *geni* 'sit'
    > Sometimes add *u*: *asma(u)* 'hear', *wagif(u)* 'stop'

3. Practice possessive phrases and 'near to' phrases together:

Bet	tomon	geriib ma	dukaan	James
Dukaan	tai	_____	bet	tai.
Medreesa	taki	_____	medereesa	taki.
_____	taniina	_____	_____	takum.
_____	takum	_____	_____	taniina.
_____	to	_____	_____	to.
_____	tomon	_____	_____	tomon.
Suk	Malakia	_____	suk	Konyo Konyo.

4. *Hasi de* 'now' means 'just' when it follows a verb, e.g., *huwo ruwa hasi
    de* 'he just went'.

5. Practice the time phrases learned so far.

Ana ruwa hasi de.	'I just went.'
Huwo safiru umbaari.	'He traveled yesterday.'
Aniina ja fi sa kamsa.	'We came at five o'clock.'
Itakum akulu gibeel.	'You ate already.'

6. *Arkabu* means both 'climb up' and 'ride'; so getting onto a vehicle and riding in it are both included.

7. *Mata* is the negative imperative 'don't'. Practice it with several verbs.

8. Using the first ten numbers and the question *Sa kam?* 'What time is it?', practice telling time. You can also use *nus* 'half', e.g., *Sa wahid u nus* '1:30'.

9. The dialogue uses *dugu bab* 'knock on door'; however, in South Sudan, people generally clap their hands outside the door or gate. This is referred to as *dugu ideen* 'clap hands'.

Kelimaat

akwaana	'brothers and/or sisters'
arkabu	'get on, ride, climb up'
ayaan	'sick'
ayaniin	'sick ones'
bab (*pl* babaat)	'door, gate'
bara	'outside, abroad'
bas (*pl* basiyaat)	'bus'
bedri	'early'
dugu	'knock, hit, clap'
fata(u)	'open'
fekiru	'think'
geni	'live, stay, sit'
geriib (ma)	'near to'
gi/ge	progressive
gofulu/gofolu	'shut, close'
hasi de	'now, just'
ideen	'hands'
ini	'here'
iyaal/yal	'children'
kadaam (*pl* kadamaat/ kadamiin)	'house worker'
kef	'how'
lori	'lorry, truck'
mata	'don't *(sg)*'

mata fekiru	'never mind'
rija	'return'
sa (saa) (*pl* sa-aat)	'hour, watch'
safiru	'travel'
umbaari	'yesterday'
wagif(u)/wogufu	'stop, stand'
yal/iyaal (sg jena)	'children'

Asilaat le temriin

1. Huwo deresu shunuu?	Huwo deresu Arabi.
2. Huwo deresu Arabi de min wen?	Huwo deresu Arabi de fi Juba.
3. Huwo arkabu shunuu?	Huwo arkabu bas.
4. Huwo arkabu bas umbaari?	La', huwo ma arkabu bas umbaari.
5. Huwo rija min wen?	Huwo rija min Yei.
6. Huwo rija min Yei ma yal to?	La', huwo ma rija min Yei ma yal to.
7. Huwo ashrubu shunuu?	Huwo ashrubu bun.
8. Huwo ashrubu bun bedri?	Ai, huwo ashrubu bun fi sa sita.
9. Humon gofulu bab?	Ai, humon gofulu bab kweis.
10. Humon gofulu bab kef?	Humon gofulu bab min bara.
11. Humon safiru le Yei?	La', humon safiru le Meridi.
12. Humon safiru le Juba fi sa talaata?	La', humon safiru le Juba fi sa arba.
13. Bas wagifu?	Ai, bas wagifu.
14. Welid de rowa hasi de?	Ai, welid de rowa hasi de ma kadaam.
15. Mara fata bab?	La', mara ma fata bab.
16. Akwaana akulu fatuur ma James?	La', humon akulu fatuur fi bet tomon.

1. Now, in pairs or around the class, using the vocabulary you have learned, ask each other questions and provide appropriate answers (not necessarily from the above sentences).

2. Practice the following questions and answers with *gi geni* 'living, staying', *ayaan* 'sick', and *fi* 'be'.

Ita gi geni wen?	Ana gi geni fi Juba.
Itakum gi geni wen?	Aniina gi geni fi Yei.
Huwo gi geni ini?	La', huwo ma gi geni ini.
Humon gi geni ini?	La', humon ma gi geni ini.
Ita ayaan?	Ai, ana ayaan.
Itakum ayaniin?	Ai, aniina ayaniin.
Huwo ayaan?	La', huwo ma ayaan.

Humon ayaniin?   La', humon ma ayaniin.
Huwo fi fi bet?   Ai, huwo fi fi bet.
Rajil fi fi bet?   Ai, huwo fi.
James fi fi bet?   Ai, huwo fi, fadal dakulu.
Mara fi fi bet?   La', huwo mafi, huwo rowa hasi de.

3. Further questions:

James gi geni wen?
James fi fi bet wala huwo safiru?
James safiru le wen?
Huwo safiru ma mara to wala la'?
Humon arkabu shunuu?
Fi zol tomon ayaan fi Yei?
Yal to fi fi bet wala humon safiru ma James?
Fi le James kadaam?
Fi le ita kadaam wala la'?
Ita gi geni wen fi Juba ini?
Ita gi dugu bab fi bet taki?
Ita gi dugu yal taki wala mara taki?
Ita gi fekiru ketiir hasi de?
Ita gi amulu shunuu hasi de?
Itakum amulu shunuu umbaari?

Deris nimira kamsa
Fi bodaboda

Lesson 5
On the motorcycle

Kalaam ma sawaag bodaboda
(A: Amiin, H: Hassan, S: sawaag)

'Dialogue with a motorcycle driver.'
(A: Amin, H: Hassan, S: 'driver')

A: Ainu, arabiiya de ma gi ruwa ta kulu kulu.

'Look, the car won't go at all.'

H: Seii ita sala makana to?

'Did you really repair its engine?'

A: Ai, ana sala makana to u ana geiru zet, lakiin batariiya karabu.

'Yes, I repaired the engine and changed the oil, but the battery is ruined.'

H: Maleesh, mata fekiru. Fi bodaboda ini.
(Huwo gi wagifu bodaboda.)

'Never mind. There are motorcycles here.'
('He stops a motorcycle.')

A: Aniina gi ruwa le jama be kam?

'How much for us to go to the university?'

S: Be arba jinee.

'For four pounds.'

A: De ketiir. Kan be itiniin jinee kweis.

'That's too much. If for two pounds, okay.'

S: La', itiniin jinee shweya.

'No, two pounds is too little.'

A: Kan be talaata jinee, kweis.

'If for three pounds, okay.'

S: Kweis, arkab.
(Humon gi arkabu u bodaboda bada ruwa.)

'Okay, get in.'
('They get in and the motorcycle begins to go.')

H: Bad siniiya lif le yamiin taki u ruwa be teriig ta zalat.

'After the roundabout turn to the right and go by the paved road.'

S: Kweis.

'Okay.'

H:	Lif le shamaal taki, badiin ruwa adiil.	'Turn to the left, then go straight.'
S:	Kweis.	'Okay.'
H:	Lif le yamiin taki be teriig ta sita biyuut.	'Turn to the right at the road of the six houses.'
S:	Kweis.	'Okay.'
H:	Yala, lif le shamaal taki u dakulu fi osh. Kalaas, wagifu ini, yauu de guruush taki.	'Turn to the left and enter into the compound. That's all, stop here. Here's your money.'
S:	Kweis, ana gi ruwa, shukran, ma salaam takum.	'Okay, I am going. Thank you. Goodbye.'
A:	Ma salaam taki.	'Goodbye.'

Kelimaat ziada al der arufu

1. Practice the phrase *ta kulu kulu* 'at all' following negative clauses:

Arabiiya	de	ma	gi ruwa	ta kulu kulu.
Lori	de	ma	gi ruwa	ta kulu kulu.
Bas	de	ma	gi ruwa	ta kulu kulu.
Ana		ma	deru ruwa	ta kulu kulu.
Aniina		ma	deriin akulu	ta kulu kulu.
Humon		ma	deriin ashrubu	ta kulu kulu.
Huwo		ma	deru esh	ta kulu kulu.
John		ma	deru laham	ta kulu kulu.

2. Practice questions using *seii*...'Is it true that...?' and positive and negative replies.

Seii ita ma deru ruwa ta kulu kulu?
      Ai, ana ma deru ruwa ta kulu kulu.
      La', ana deru ruwa.
Seii itakum ma deriin akulu laham ta kulu kulu?
      Ai, aniina ma deriin akulu laham ta kulu kulu.
      La', aniina deriin akulu laham.
Seii ita ma derisu Arabi ta kulu kulu?
      Ai, ana ma derisu Arabi ta kulu kulu.
      La', ana derisu Arabi.
Seii ita lisa ma safiru le Yei ta kulu kulu?
      Ai, ana ma safiru le Yei ta kulu kulu.
      La', ana safiru le Yei.
Seii ita lisa ma ainu Yei ta kulu kulu?

Seii   ita lisa ma fata bab?
                    gofulu bab?
                    arkabu lori?
Seii   ita kan ma ayaan ta kulu kulu? (or ma kan ayaan)
        Ai, ana ma kan ayaan ta kulu kulu.
        La', ana kan ayaan.
Seii   yal taki ma kan ayaaniin ta kulu kulu?
        Ai, yal tai ma kan ayaaniin ta kulu kulu.
        La', yal tai kan ayaaniin.
Seii   ita derisu Arabi?
                    ruwa le suk aleela?
                    sala makana ta arabiiya?
                    geiru zet ta lori?
                    geiru batariiya ta arabiiya taki?
                    dugu akwaana taki?

3. *Kan* was previously used in a single clause to mean 'was', e.g., *Ana kan ayaan*
    or *kan ana ayaan* 'I was sick'. In this lesson, it means 'if, when' when it oc-
    curs in a conditional clause, e.g., *Kan be itiniin jinee, kweis* 'If for two pounds,
    good'; *Kan ita ruwa be bodaboda, ma bataal* 'If you go by motorcycle, that's
    not bad'; *Kan huwo nagisu shweya, ma bataal* 'If he reduces the price a little,
    not bad'; or *Huwo rija le bet, kan ayaan* 'He returned home when sick.'

4. Arabic nouns can be collective, singular, or plural. The most common
    collective nouns cannot be counted, e.g., *moya* 'water'; however, others
    can be counted, e.g., *esh* 'bread'. In Juba Arabic a great many singular
    nouns are used in a plural sense, as if they were collective nouns. The
    plural forms are used more by educated speakers. It is common to hear
    haja ketiir 'many things' or *talaata oda* 'three rooms', but it is "more
    correct" to say *hajaat ketiir* or *talaata odaat*.

    Most plural nouns end in *-aat*, some end in *-iin*, some can end in ei-
    ther, and some are irregular (involving stem changes).

    a. Examples of nouns ending in *-aat*:

bab, babaat	'door'
defaan, defanaat	'guest'
dukaan, dukanaat	'shop'
gufa, gufaat	'basket'
haja, hajaat	'thing'
kadaam, kadamaat	'house worker'
kubaaya, kubayaat	'cup'
mara, mariaat	'woman'

suk, sukaat	'market'
terebeeza, terebezaat	'table'
zabuun, zabunaat	'customer'

. When a stressed suffix, such as -*aat,* is added to a word already having a double vowel, the previous double vowel is reduced to a single vowel because stress is shifted to the last syllable, e.g., *jawaab* followed by -*aat* becomes *jawabaat* 'letters'.

Nouns ending in *s* insert *i* before -*aat,* e.g., *deris, derisiaat; kis, kisiaat; mudeeris, muderisiaat.*

    b.   Examples of nouns ending in -*iin:*

mudeeris, muderisiin	'teacher'
sawaag, sawagiin	'driver'
Januub Sudaani, Januub Sudaniin	'South Sudanese'

    c.   Examples of nouns with irregular stem changes:

bet, biyuut	'house'
rajil, rujaliin	'man'
welid, awlaad	'boy'
yom, ayaam	'day'
zerif, zeruuf	'envelope'

5.   Practice giving and receiving directions:

Min maktab ta ruwa le hadi teriig ta zalat.
Badiin lif le shamaal taki u ruwa adiil le hadi siniiya ta Mobil.
Badiin lif siniiya le shamaal taki.
Badiin ruwa adiil le hadi Malakia.
Badiin ita gi ainu suk Malakia.
Min suk Malakia rija le teriig ta zalat.
Badiin lif le yamiin taki u ruwa adiil le hadi siniiya ta Mobil, u lif le yamiin taki.
Badiin ruwa adiil le hadi teriig nimira wahid.
Lif le yamiin taki u ruwa adiil.
Wagifu ini.
Yauu de, maktab ta medereesa fi yamiin taki.

6.   *Le hadi* 'until' was introduced above, along with *maktab* 'office'. Other words to practice in giving directions are *gidaam* 'ahead' and *wara* 'behind'.

7. Prepositions sometimes occur in pairs, e.g., *geriib ma dukaan* 'near to the store' or *geriib min bab* 'near to the door'. When used as subordinating conjunctions, *ma* is obligatory, e.g., *bad ma akulu* 'after eating' or *geriib ma ruwa* 'about to go'.

8. In Juba Arabic, *defaan, defanaat* is used more commonly for 'visitor' than *def, diyuuf.*

9. *Badiin* and *badeen* 'then' are both common, but *badeen* is more common in the city.

Kelimaat

adiil	'straight'
aleela	'today'
arabiiya	'car'
awlaad (sg weled)	'boys, sons, children'
ayaam (sg yom)	'days'
bad ma	'after'
bada(u)	'begin'
badiin/badeen	'then'
batariiya, batariiyaat	'battery'
biyuut (sg bet)	'houses'
bodaboda	'motorcycle'
def (pl diyuuf)	'guest, visitor'
geiru	'change'
geriib ma	'about to'
gidaam	'ahead'
jama	'university'
Januub Sudaan	'South Sudan'
Januub Sudaani (pl Januub Sudaniin)	'South Sudanese' (n)
kan (conj)	'if, when'
kan (v)	'was/were'
karabu	'ruined'
kubaaya (pl kubayaat)	'cup, glass'
le hadi/li hadi	'until'
lifu	'turn'
makana (pl makanaat)	'engine'
maktab (pl maktabaat)	'office'
maleesh	'sorry, never mind'
mudeeris (pl mudeerisiin/ mudeerisiat)	'teacher'

nahaar de	'today'
osh	'compound, yard'
sala(u)	'repair'
sawaag (*pl* sawagiin)	'driver'
seii	'Is it true that...?'
shamaal	'left, north'
siniiya	'roundabout'
ta kulu kulu	'at all'
terebeeza (*pl* terebezaat)	'table'
teriig	'road, way'
wara	'behind'
yala	'hey'
yamiin	'right (not left)'
yom (*pl* ayaam)	'day'
zalat	'asphalt'
zerif (*pl* zeruuf)	'envelope'

Asilaat le muraaja min de-ris nimira wahid le kamsa

Review questions from lessons 1–5

1. Ita akulu fatuur fi sa tamaanya nahaar de?
2. Kadaam gi ruwa wen?
3. Ita akulu samaga fi suk Kongo Kongo?
4. James arkabu bas fi sa kam?
5. Sidu dukaan gofulu dukaan kan akulu fatuur?
6. Rajil de deru shunuu?
7. Ita deru bun wala shay?
8. Ita alimu Arabi ini?
9. Itakum gi ruwa fi bet hasi de?
10. Yal taki ayaniin?
11. Sa kam hasi de?
12. Akwaana taki ruwa min Yei umbaari?
13. Fi esh u laham fi terebeeza?
14. Itakum gi geni fi teriig de?
15. Sawaag sala arabiiya taki? (ta Amiin?)
16. Shay amuluu kalaas?
17. Fi siniiya geriib min ini?
18. Arabiiya ta Amiin kweis wala bataal?
19. Mahaal ta fawaaki geriib ma mahaal shunuu?
20. Kilo sukar be kam hasi de?
21. Ita deru ruwa le suk ma John? (ma Tereesa?)
22. Itakum deriin akulu fatuur wala itakum deriin ashrubu shay?
23. John kan ayaan umbaari?

24. Kan John ayaan, kweis?
25. Ita deru rija le bet?
26. Ita gi geni fi bet de hasi de?
27. Makana ta arabiiya taki kweis wala bataal?
28. Batariiya ta arabiiya tomon kweis wala karabu?
29. Kan arabiiya karabu, kweis?
30. Kan manga be kamsa guruush, kweis?
31. Fi shunuu gidaam taki? (wara taki?)
32. Fi shunuu gidaam Pam? (wara Pam?)
33. Ian gi geni fi yamiin taki wala fi shamaal taki?
34. Pam gi geni wen? fi yamiin taki?
35. Fi kadaam fi bet taki wala mafi?
36. Bet taki wenu?
37. Bet ta Keith fi osh?
38. Bab de fatauu wala gofuluu?

Deris nimira sita
Fi kuluub

Lesson 6
At the restaurant

Kalaam fi kuluub
(R: rajil, J: jarasoon, M: mara)

'Dialogue in a restaurant'
(R: 'man', J: 'waiter', M: 'woman')

R: Fi mahaal fadi?

'Is there an empty place?'

J: Ai, fi terebeeza dak geriib min bab dak.

'Yes, there is a table near that door.'

R: (le mara) Terebeeza de kweis?

'(to the woman) Is this table okay?'

M: La', terebeeza de geriib min bab. Dak yauu kweis.

'No, this table is too near the door. That one there is okay.'

R: Kweis, geni. Ita deru moya?

'Good, sit down. Do you want water?'

M: Ana deru moya lemuun.

'I want lemonade.'

R: (le jarasoon) Asma, ita, jibu itiniin moya lemuun.

'(to waiter) Listen, you, bring two lemonades.'

J: Kweis, ya sabi. Itakum deriin asha?

'Yes sir. Do you want supper?'

R: Ai, fi waraga ta akilaat de?

'Yes, is there a menu?'

J: Ai, fi.
(Badiin huwo gi jibu waraga ta akilaat.)

'Yes there is.'
('Then he brings a menu.')

M: Fi samaga muhaamur?

'Is there fried fish?'

J: Ai, ya mara.

'Yes, madam.'

R: (le mara) Ita akulu kabaab ini? Kabaab ini kweis kalis.

'(to the woman) Have you eaten a kabob here? A kabob here is very good.'

M: Kweis, ana deru kabaab u bataatis muhaamur u salata.

'Good, I want a kabob and fried potatoes, and salad.'

43

R: Ana deru shurba u kibda be bed gidaada.

'I want soup and liver with eggs.'

J: Yani, itakum deriin wahid kebaab be bataatis muhaamur u wahid shurba u wahid kibda be bed gidaada. Aleela aniina ma amulu salata.

'That means you want one kabob with fried potatoes and one soup, and one liver with eggs. Today we haven't made salad.'

(Badiin jarasoon gi jibu akil.)

('Then the waiter brings the food.')

M: Akil de kweis kalis, muze de?

'This food is very delicious, isn't it?'

R: Ai, kweis kalis shediid.

'Yes, very, very delicious.'

R: Ya jarasoon, taal ini. (Jarasoon gi ja.)

'Waiter, come here.'

('The waiter comes.')

R: Akil al aniina akulu de kulu be kam?

'The food which we ate totals how much?'

J: Kulu be saba jinee.

'Seven pounds altogether.'

R: Yauu de guruush taki.

'Here is your money.'

M: Guruush de ketiir kalis.

'That's expensive.'

R: Kweis, aniina gi ruwa. Ma salaam taki.

'Okay, we are going. Goodbye.'

Kelimaat ziada al der arufu

1. Practice asking questions following the examples given.

    De samaga?   Ai, de samaga; samaga de kweis kalis.
    De laham?   Ai, de laham; laham de kweis kalis.
    De bed gidaada?
    De kabaab?
    De shurba?
    De kibda?
    De salata?
    De bun?
    etc.

2. Practice the negative response, as follows:

    Samaga de kweis?   La', samaga de ma kweis.
    etc.

3. Practice the comparative construction, as follows:

Samaga dak kweis kalis min sa- maga de. Laham dak kweis kalis min la- ham de. etc.	'That fish is better than this fish' 'That meat is better than this meat.'

Next, the teacher can alternate between the above statements and the reverse, state *Samaga de kweis kalis min samaga dak* and have the students reply with *Kweis, jibu le ana samaga de* or *dak,* as appropriate.

4. The imperative uses the pronouns *ita, itakum,* or *aniina.* However, the pronoun can be omitted as with *jibu* in the drill above. Also, a vocative can be inserted between the pronoun and the verb, e.g., *ita, ya welid, ruwa fi bet* 'you, boy, go home.' Practice the following commands:

Asma, ita, jibu moya. bun shay lemuun etc.	Asma, itakum, jibu moya le aniina. bun shay lemuun etc.

5. Negative commands are formed with *mata* 'don't' or *matakum* 'don't (you all)'. Practice the following:

Asma, ita mata jibu moya.
          bun
          etc.
Mata ainu arabiiya dak.
  ruwa le bet
  etc.
	Asma, matakum jibu moya le aniina.
	          bun
	          etc.
	Matakum ainu arabiiya dak.
	  ruwa le bet.
	  etc.

6. Learn numbers eleven and twelve *(hidaasher, itnaasher)* and the fractions *rubu* 'quarter' and *tilit* 'third', which are used extensively, like *nus* 'half', in telling time.

3:15	talaata u rubu
3:20	talaata u tilit
3:30	talaata u nus
3:40	arba ila tilit
3:45	arba ila rubu

7. When counting items beyond 10, the singular (base) form of a noun is used. Plural forms are used only with numbers 2–10, if at all.

Kelimaat

akil	'food'
akil (*pl* akilaat)	'meal'
al	'who/which'
dak	'that'
fadi	'free, empty'
hidaasher	'eleven'
ila	'less, minus'
itnaasher	'twelve'
jarasoon (*pl* jarasonaat)	'waiter'
kabaab	'beef kabob'
kibda (*pl* kindaat)	'liver'
kulu	'altogether'
kuluub	'restaurant'
matakum	'don't (*pl*)'
muhaamur	'fried'
muze (de)?	'isn't that so?'
rubu	'one fourth'
sabi	'sir'
salata	'salad'
shediid	'very'
shurba	'soup'
tilit	'one third'
waraga	'paper'
waraga ta akilaat	'menu'
yani	'that means'
yauu	'specifically'

Asilaat le temriin

1. Fi mahaal fadi fi kuluub?
2. Terebeeza fi kuluub de kweis?
3. Terebeeza wenu yauu kweis?
4. Mara deru moya shunuu?
5. Jarasoon jibu moya lemuun kam kubaaya?
6. Jarasoon yauu deru asha?
7. Waraga ta akilaat yani shunuu be Ingliizi?
8. Ita akulu samaga muhaamur fi Juba?
9. Ita akulu kabaab fi Juba?
10. Mara deru akil shunuu?
11. Rajil deru akil shunuu?
12. Jarasoon kelimu shunuu le humon?

13. Aleela ma amuluu shunuu fi kuluub?
14. Akil al humon akulu kan kweis kalis shediid?
15. Akil al humon akulu kulu be kam jinee?
16. Ita akulu kabaab muhaamur fi bet taki?
17. Bed gidaada be salata kweis min bed gidaada be bataatis?
18. Akil al ita akulu fi fatuur muze kweis?
19. Itakum akulu gada fi sa kam umbaari?
20. Sa arba ila rubu yani sa talaata u kam degiiga?

Deris nimira saba
Fi bet

Kalaam fi bet
(U: uma, M: Maria, J: John)

U: Ya Maria, yal wenu?
M: John gi geni fi oda juluus u James gi geni alabu bara.
U: John gi geni amulu shunuu fi oda juluus?
M: Huwo gi geni katibu.
U: Kweis, ita gatau bataatis de?
M: Ai, ana gatau bataatis de u ana gi kasulu afashaat.
U: Kweis, ana gi ruwa le suk.
    (John gi jibu waraga le uma to.)
J: Ya mama, ana resemu samaga. Ainu, mama, de bahar u de samaga fi bahar.
U: Ai, ita shatir. Kamaan ita katibu haja tani?
J: Ana katibu de kulu, lakiin galam karabu. Jibu le ana galam tani min dukaan, ya mama.
U. Kweis, ana bi jibu le ita.

Lesson 7
At home

'Dialogue at home'
(U: 'mother', M: Mary, J: John)

'Mary, where are the children?'
'John is sitting in the parlor and James is playing outside.'
'What is John doing in the parlor?'

'He is sitting, writing.'
'Good, have you cut up the potatoes?'
'Yes, I have cut up the potatoes and I am washing the dishes.'
'Good, I am going to the market.'
('John brings a paper to his mother.')
'I drew a fish. Look, this is the river and this is the fish in the river.'

'Yes, you are clever. Did you also write anything else?'
'I wrote all of this, but the pen is ruined. Bring me another pen from the store, mama.'
'Okay, I will bring you one.'

49

Kelimaat ziada al der arufu

1. Practice the following sentences with the future or indefinite marker *bi*.

Uma ta Maria bi ruwa le suk.	'Mary's mother will go to market.'
Uma ta welid bi jibu galam.	'The boy's mother will bring a pen.'
Ana bi derisu Arabi kulu yom.	'I will study Arabic every day.'
Aniina bi akulu fatuur kulu yom.	'We will eat breakfast every day.'
Humon bi rija le Meriidi bukra.	'They will return to Maridi tomorrow.'
Humon bi ruwa le Yei fi shahar de.	'They will go to Yei this month.'
Huwo bi welidu jena fi usbuu de.	'She will give birth to a child this week.'

    Bad aniina derisu Arabi, aniina bi ruwa le bet.
    Bad aniina ashrubu shay, aniina bi ruwa le medereesa.
    Bad aniina akulu fatuur, aniina bi ruwa le maktab.
    Bad sa itniin aniina bi akulu gada.
    Bad sa tamaanya aniina bi akulu asha.
    Bad sa tisa aniina bi akulu fatuur.

2. Practice questions and answers with *bi* 'future, indefinite' and the question word *miteen* 'when'.

Ita bi ruwa le suk miteen?	'When will you go to market?'
Ana bi ruwa le suk fi sa saba.	'I will go to market at seven o'clock.'
Ita bi ruwa le Meriidi miteen?	'When will you go to Maridi?'
Ana bi ruwa le Meriidi fi yom wahid.	'I'll go to Maridi on the first.'
Ita bi safiru le Ameerika miteen?	'When will you go to America?'
Ana bi safiru le Ameerika fi usbuu de.	'I'll go to America this week.'
Ita be safiru le Britaanya miteen?	'When will you go to Britain?'
Ana bi safiru le Britaanya fi shahar de.	'I'll go to Britain this month.'
Ita be amulu bun miteen?	'When will you make coffee?'
Ana bi amulu bun fi sa ashara.	'I'll make coffee at ten o'clock.'
Ita bi kasulu afashaat miteen?	'When will you wash the dishes?'
Ana bi kasulu afashaat fi sa kamsa.	'I'll wash the dishes at five o'clock.'

3. *Yom wahid,* like the longer form *yom wahid fi shahar,* means 'the first day of the month'. All the days of a month are counted in this way. Days of the week are taught in lesson 16.

4. Practice the following commands by obeying them.

    Amulu hasab mudeeris kelimu. 'Do according to what the teacher tells you.'
    Ya ____,   wagifu fog!
    Ya ____,   geni teet!
    Ya ____,   ruwa le bab!
                fata bab!
                gofulu bab!
                dugu bab!
                lif le shamaal taki!
                lif le yamiin taki!
                ruwa adiil!
                rija fi mahaal taki!
                jibu le ana moya!
                jibu le Keith moya tani!
                taal ini!
                ruwa bara!
                dakulu tani!
                wagifu fog badiin ruwa le bab!
                rija le mahaal taki badiin geni teet!
                fata bab badiin gofulu tani!
                lif le yamiin taki badiin ruwa adiil!
                lif le yamiin taki tani u taal geni teet
                bad deris jibu waraga takum wa rija le maktab takum!

5. *Bi* (future/indefinite time) is used in a main clause following a condi-
    tional clause, e.g., *Kan huwo ayaan, huwo ma bi akulu.* 'When/if he is
    sick, he doesn't/won't eat'. Practice making other sentences with *Kan...*
    and *bi....*

Kelimaat

afash (*pl* afashaat)	'dish'
alabu	'play'
Ameerika	'America'
bahar/baar	'river, sea'
bi	future/indefinite
Britaanya	'Britain'
bukra	'tomorrow'
fog	'up, above'
galam (*pl* galamaat)	'pen, pencil'
gatau	'cut'
hasab	'according to'

jena (*pl* yal)	'child'
juluus; oda juluus	'parlor, living room'
kasulu	'wash'
katibu	'write/wrote'
kelimu	'say, tell'
mama	'mama, mommy'
miteen	'when'
oda (*pl* odaat)	'room'
resemu/resimu	'draw'
shatir	'clever, intelligent'
tehet/teet	'down, below, under'
uma (*pl* umahaat)	'mother'
usbuu	'week'
welidu	'give birth'

Asilaat le temriin

1. Uma ta Maria kelimu shunuu le Maria?
2. John gi geni fi oda wen?
3. James gi geni amulu shunuu?
4. John gi geni amulu shunuu fi oda?
5. Uma ta John gatau bataatis u kasulu afashaat?
6. Uma ta John ruwa le wen?
7. John resemu shunuu?
8. John kelimu shunuu le uma to?
9. Shunuu yauu karabu le John?
10. Uma ta John kelimu shunuu le John?
11. Ita alabu yom tani fi bahar wala la'?
12. Bet taki fi kam odaat?
13. Ita be resemu kweis?
14. Fi mara bi welidu fi usbuu de?
15. Jena taki shatir?
16. Bad ma yal taki akulu asha, humon bi amulu shunuu?
17. Ita kulu yom bi ruwa le suk fi sa kam?
18. Bad ma yal taki ashrubu shay fi sabaa, humon bi amulu shunuu?
19. Ita kulu yom bi rija min maktab le bet fi sa kam?
20. Kam galam taki karabu, ita bi amulu shunuu?
21. Ita bi akulu asha fi sa kam?
22. Ita bi akulu fatuur fi sa kam?
23. Ita bi alabu fi sa kam?
24. Fi samaga kebiir fi bahar?
25. Ita deru shurba be samaga wala be kibda?

Deris nimira tamaanya   Lesson 8
Ma jeraan   With a neighbor

Kalaam ma jeraan

(S: Januub Sudaani, K: kawaaja)

'Dialogue with a neighbor'

(S: 'South Sudanese', K: 'foreigner')

S: Salaam taki.

K: Ahlen, salaam taki.

S: Rabuuna kelii saaidu ita.

K: Kef ita?

S: Kweis, itakum gi geni ini?

K: Ai, aniina gi geni fi bet de.

S: Ya salaam, aniina jeraan. Ana gi geni fi sharia dak. Itakum geni kam shahar fi Januub Sudaan ini?

K: Wahid usbuu bes.

S: Geriib. Juba kweis?

K: Kweis kalis. Ita min beled de zatu?

S: La', weliduu ana fi Yei, lakiin ana geni fi Juba le muda ishriin sena. Wa ita min wen?

K: Ana min Britaanya.

S: Ana asmau Britaanya beled kweis Jibuu ita le shokol shunuu fi Juba ini?

K: Jibuu ana ashaan derisu fi jama. Seii ita arifu Jama Juba?

'Hello.'

'Welcome. Hello.'

'May the Lord help you.'

'How are you?'

'Fine, do you live here?'

'Yes, we are living in this house.'

'Heavens, we are neighbors. I live in that street. How many months have you lived here in South Sudan?'

'Only one week.'

'Very recent. Is Juba good?'

'Very good. Are you a native of this very village?'

'No, I was born in Yei, but I have been living in Juba for twenty years. And where are you from?'

'I'm from Britain.'

'I've heard that Britain is a nice country. What work brings you here to Juba?'

'I was brought to teach in the university. Do you know Juba University?'

S: Lazim. Mara taki shagaal kamaan?
'Of course. Does your wife work also? (lit. Is your wife also a worker?)'

K: Ai, huwo sikirteer fi Umam al Muteeheda. U ita shagaal mu-waazif?
'Yes, she is a secretary at the United Nations. And are you an office worker?'

S: La', ana makaniiki al gi sala ara-biyaat. Izin taki, ana deru ruwa le shokol. Aniina bi limu fi wokit tani. Ma salaam taki.
'No, I am a mechanic who repairs cars. Excuse me, I want to go to work. We will meet at another time. Goodbye.'

K: Ma salaam taki kamaan.
'Goodbye to you too.'

Kelimaat ziada al der arufu

1. There are two additions to the greetings previously learned. First is *Rabuuna kelii saaidu ita* 'May the Lord help you', which is similar to the Arabic *Allah yibaarik fiik* 'God bless you'. The second is *Kef ita?* or *Ita kef?* 'How are you?'

2. A few of the most common questions South Sudanese ask foreigners are:

Ita min wen?	'Where are you from?'
Beled taki wenu?	'Where is your country?'
Ita geni kam shahar fi Januub Sudaan?	'How many months have you lived in South Sudan?'

3. Another common question introduces a new sentence order:

Jibuu ita le shokol shunuu?	'For what work were you brought?'
Jibuu ana ashaan deresu.	'I was brought in order to teach.'
Weliduu ana fi Yei.	'I was born in Yei.'

   This is a passive construction without any stated agent, and the subject (logical object) follows the verb. Compare *fatuur amuluu* 'breakfast is made' in lesson 3.

4. *Izin taki* 'excuse me; with your permission' is a polite expression used when wanting to speak to someone who is busy, when passing through a crowd, or when breaking off a visit, as in the dialogue here.

5. Another construction (first used in lesson 6) is the relative clause used to modify a noun. The relative pronoun is *al* 'who, which'.

Umam al Muteeheda	'nations which are united (i.e., United Nations)'
makaniiki al gi sala arabiyaat	'A mechanic who repairs cars'
akil al aniina akulu de	'the food which we ate'

6. Notice that *deresu* means either 'study' or 'teach'. Only the context can clarify which meaning is intended. If you hear *Ana deresu Arabi,* you must look to see if the speaker appears to be an Arabic speaker or learner. But if you hear *Ana deresu John,* you can be certain that the speaker is the teacher.

7. With your teacher's help, make up a short dialogue about yourself based on the one in this lesson. Then, memorize it and use it in conversation with South Sudanese friends and neighbors.

Kelimaat

ashaan	'in order to'
beled	'country, village'
bes	'only'
deresu/derisu	'study, teach'
geriib	'recent'
ishriin	'twenty'
izin taki	'excuse me'
jeraan (*pl* jeranaat)	'neighbor'
jibuu	'was brought'
kawaaja (*pl* kawajaat)	'foreigner'
kelii	'may'
lazim	'of course, certainly'
limu	'meet'
makaniiki	'mechanic'
muteeheda	'united'
muwaazif	'employee, worker, official'
Rabuuna	'Lord'
saaidu	'help' (*v*)
sena	'year'
shagaal	'worker'
sharia	'street'
shokol	'work' (*n*)
sikirteer	'secretary'
umam	'nations'
Umam Al Muteeheda	'United Nations'
weliduu	'born'

wokit	'time, occasion'
ya salaam	'good heavens!'
zatu	'this very' (emphasis)

Asilaat le temriin

1. Kef ita?
2. Ita gi geni wen fi Juba ini?
3. Kawaaja de geni kam shahar fi Januub Sudaan ini?
4. Zol Januub Sudaani de geni jeraan ma itakum?
5. Zol Januub Sudaani de weliduu wen?
6. Zol Januub Sudaani de geni kam sena fi Juba?
7. Beled ta kawaaja de wenu?
8. Jibuu kawaaja de ashaan shokol shunuu fi Januub Sudaan ini?
9. Kawaaja de mara to shagaal shunuu?
10. Mara ta kawaaja de shagaal fi Jama Juba wala shagaal fi Umam al Muteeheda?
11. Mara ta kawaaja de shagaal shokol shunuu fi Umam al Muteeheda?
12. Januub Sudaani de shagaal shokol shunuu?
13. Makaniiki gi sala shunuu kulu yom?
14. Weliduu ita wen?
15. Ita shagaal shokol shunuu hasi de?
16. Ita kan deresu Arabi?
17. Ita kulu yom bi limu ma jeraan taki wen?
18. Ita deru saaidu yal taki wala nas kulu?
19. Ita gi sala arabiiya taki kan karabu?
20. Beled taki kweis kalis min Januub Sudaan?

Deris nimira tisa
Fi maktab busta[1]

Lesson 9
At the post office

Kalaam fi maktab busta
(L: Lela, M: Muna, K: katib)

'Dialogue at the post office'
(L: Lela, M: Muna, K: 'clerk')

L: Ya Muna, ana katibu jawaab ini. Ita gi ruwa le maktab busta?

'Muna, I have written this letter. Are you going to the post office?'

M: Ai, ana bi ruwa bad shweya. Maktab busta bi gofolu fi sa itnaasher, muze de?

'Yes, I'll go in a little while. The post office will close at noon, isn't that so?'

L: Degiiga. Lazim ana dakulu jawaab de fi zerif wa katibu anwaan.

'Wait a minute. I must put this letter into an envelope and write the address.'

M: Teb. Dauud selemu jawabaat min senduuk umbaari?

'Okay. Did David collect the letters from the box yesterday?'

L: La', huwo woduru muftaa. Lakiin fi muftaa tani ini.
(fi maktab busta)

'No, he lost the key. But there is another key here.'
('at the post office')

M: Ana deru tamaanya tawaabe min abu sita jinee wa talaata min abu arba jinee, wa talaata jawabaat al gi ruwa be tiyaara.

'I want eight stamps of six pounds, three of four pounds, and three airforms.'

K: Kweis, ya mara.

'Yes, ma'am.'

M: Mumkin ana bi sejilu jawaab bita-ai ini?

'Is it possible for me to register my letter here?'

---

[1] These lessons were first written in 1985, which explains why some lessons—particularly this one—are somewhat dated. Nevertheless, they have been retained for their grammar and vocabulary.

K: La', fi safa dak fi yamiin taki.   'No, in that section on your right.'
M: Shukran.   'Thank you.'
   (Huwo sejilu jawaab u jibu zerif al   ('She registers the letter and takes
   kebiir le safa ta zerif al kebiir.)   the parcel to the parcel section.')
M: Asma, ita, ana deru rasulu zerif al   'Listen please, I want to send this
   kebiir de le Ameerika be beriid al   parcel to America by surface mail.
   adi. De be kam?   How much is this?'
K: Haja de hasab wazin. Wazin to tala   'This thing is according to weight.
   itniin kilo. Dafau talaata jinee.   Its weight exceeds two kilos. Pay
                                                three pounds.'
M: Shukran. Ma salaam taki.   'Thank you. Goodbye.'
K: Ma salaam taki kamaan.   'Goodbye to you too.'

Kelimaat ziada al der arufu

1. *Lazim,* translated 'of course, certainly' in the last lesson, usually pre-
    cedes or follows the subject of a clause and is translated 'must, have
    to'. It is typically used with *gi* for present tense or immediate future, or
    with *bi* for future. Practice the following sentences:

    Lazim ana gi ruwa le suk.   'I must be going to the market.'
    Lazim ana bi ruwa le Yei.   'I must be going to Yei.'
    Lazim ana bi dafau guruush.   'I must pay money.'
    Lazim ana __ arkabu bas.   'I must ride the bus.'
    Lazim ana __fatau bab.   'I must open the door.'
    Lazim ana __kasulu afashaat.   'I must wash the dishes.'
    Lazim ana __safiru le Meriidi.   'I must travel to Maridi.'

2. *Mumkin* 'possible' is a modal which usually precedes the subject or
    stands alone, meaning 'is it possible?' or 'it is possible'. Practice the fol-
    lowing sentences.

    Mumkin ita bi ruwa le suk?   'Can you go to the market?'
    Ma mumkin ana bi ruwa le suk.   'It's not possible for me to go to the
                                        market.'

    Mumkin ita kelii huwo sala   'Can you let him repair the motor?'
    makana?
    Ai, kelii huwo salau.   'Yes, let him repair it.'
    La', mata kelii huwo salau.   'No, don't let him repair it.'
    Mumkin huwo sala makana?   'Is it possible for him to repair the
                                        engine?'

    Ai, mumkin.   'Yes, it's possible.'
    La', ma mumkin.   'No, it's not possible.'

Ana ma bi kelii huwo sala maka-   'I won't let him repair the motor.
na. Huwo bi karabu.   He will ruin it.'

3. *Degiiga* means 'a minute' or 'wait a minute'. In the latter case, it is usu-
    ally said with a hand motion, or may be communicated by the hand
    motion alone. Practice the following sentences with *degiiga*.

    Degiiga, ana deru...   'Wait a minute, I want to...'
        katibu jawaab.   'write a letter.'
        dakulu jawaab fi zerif.   'put the letter into the
                                          envelope.'
        katibu anwaan fi zerif.   'write the address on the
                                          envelope.'
        resemu senduuk.   'draw a box.'
        rasulu senduuk.   'send a box.'
        rasulu zerif al kebiir.   'send a parcel.'
        sejilu.   'register.'
        selemu guruush.   'collect money.'
        dafau guruush.   'pay money.'
        ruwa le maktab busta.   'go to the post office.'

4. *Dakulu* 'enter' can be used as a causative verb 'put into', just as *deresu*
    can be 'study' or 'teach' (i.e., 'cause to study').

5. *Abu* means 'kind of', e.g., *abu sita jinee* 'the six pound kind', *abu kweis*
    'the good kind', and *abu wahid* 'the same kind'.

    Jibu abu kweis, mata jibu abu bataal. 'Bring the good kind, not the bad
                                           kind.'
    Jibu talaata min abu de.   'Bring three of this kind.'

    Abu can also be used in nicknames, e.g., *abu sala* 'bald man', or *abu digin*
    'bearded man'.

6. Practice the following sentences with *asma ita* 'listen please':

        Asma ita, ana deru...   'Listen please, I want...'
        muftaa ta bet.   'the housekey.'
        muftaa ta senduuk.   'the mailbox key.'
        anwaan taki.   'your address.'
        zerif ta jawaab.   'the envelope of the letter.'
        senduuk fi maktab busta.   'a mailbox.'
        tabe min abu ashara jinee.   'a ten-pound stamp.'

itniin tawaabe min abu kamsa jinee.   'two five-pound stamps.'

kamsa jawaab al gi ruwa be tiyaara.   'five airforms.'

7.   Practice the following questions:

Lela amulu shunuu fi bet?   'What was Lela doing at home?'
Lela dakulu jawaab fi shunuu?
Muna bi ruwa le wen?
Maktab busta bi gofulu fi sa kam kulu yom?
Dauud amulu shunuu umbaari?
Muftaa tani wenu?
Muna deru kam tawaabe kulu?
Muna deru kam jawabaat al gi ruwa be tiyaara?
Fi kam safaat fi maktab busta?
Muna deru rasulu zerif al kebiir le wen?
Muna deru rasulu zerif al kebiir be tiyaara wala be beriid al adi?
Zerif al kebiir ta Muna wazin to kam kilo?
Huwo dafau kam jinee?
Katib fi safa ta tawaabe be sejilu jawaab?
Senduuk takum fi maktab busta nimira to kam?
Itakum deriin jawabaat wala zerif al kebiir?
Wazin taki kam kilo?

8.   *Degiiga* 'minute' and its plural *degaayg* 'minutes' can now be used for telling the time when minutes are needed other than *rubu, tilit,* and *nus.*

Hasi de sa kam?
Hasi de sa tamaanya u kamsa degaayg.
Hasi de sa tamaanya u nus ila kamsa degaayg.
Hasi de sa tamaanya u ashara degaayg.

Hasi de sa tamaanya u nus u kamsa degaayg.
Hasi de sa tisa ila ashara degaayg.
Hasi de sa tisa ila kamsa degaayg.

Kelimaat

abu	'kind of'
anwaan	'address' *(n)*
asma ita	'listen please'
bad(i) shweya	'in a little while'

beriid al adi	'surface mail'
busta	'post (office)'
dafau	'pay'
dakulu	'cause to enter, put into'
Dauud	'David'
degaayg	'minutes'
degiiga	'(wait) a minute'
digin	'beard'
jawaab (*pl* jawabaat)	'letter, answer'
jawaab al gi ruwa be tiyaara	'airform, air letter'
katib	'clerk'
kebiir	'big, large'
kelii	'let'
lazim	'must, have to'
maktab busta	'post office'
muftaa (*pl* muftahaat)	'key'
mumkin	'possible'
rasulu	'send'
safa (*pl* safaat)	'section, line, queue'
sala	'bald'
sejilu	'register'
selemu	'collect'
senduuk (*pl* sendukaat)	'box'
tabe (*pl* tawaabe)	'stamp'
tala	'go out, go over, exceed'
teb	'okay'
tiyaara (*pl* tiyaraat)	'airplane'
wahid/waid	'same'
wazin	'weight'
woduru	'lose, lost'
zerif al kebiir	'parcel, large envelope'

Deris nimira ashara
Fi hisa Arabi

Lesson 10
At Arabic class

Kalaam fi hisa Arabi
(M: mudeeris, K: kulu, P: Paul,
J: John, E: Elizabeth, S: Suzaan)

'Dialogue in the Arabic class'
(M: 'teacher', K: 'all', P: Paul,
J: John, E: Elizabeth, S: Suzanne)

M: Itakum num kef?

'How are you? (lit. How did you sleep?)'

K: Aniina kulu num kweisiin.

'We all are fine this morning. (lit. We all slept well.)'

M: Itakum zekiru deris ta umbaari de?

'Have you memorized yesterday's lesson?'

P: Ai, aniina zekiru, lakiin aniina ma afamu kweis kelima de.

'Yes, we memorized it, but we don't understand this word well.'

M: Kelima shunuu?

'What word?'

P: Kelima 'safa'.

'The word safa.'

M: Itakum ma arifu kelima 'safa'? Fi maktab busta fi safaat ketiir. Fi safa ta tawaabe, u fi safa ta jawabaat, u kida. Itakum famu hasi de?

'You don't know the word safa? At the post office there are many sections. There is a stamp section, a letter section, etc. Do you understand now?'

P: Ai, shukran.

'Yes, thank you.'

M: Fi asila tani?

'Is there another question?'

J: Ai, ana ma arifu kelima paper be Arabi.

'Yes, I don't know the word 'paper' in Arabic.'

M: Paper mana to 'waraga'.

"Paper' means waraga.'

J: Kan ta asma, kelim tani.

'If you will, say it again.'

M: Waraga. Mumkin ita bagder katibu 'waraga' fi sobuura?

'Can you write waraga on the blackboard?'

J: De sah?   'Is it right?'

M: Ai, sah. Ita katibu kweis. Ya Elizabeth,   'Yes, correct. You write well. Eliz-
   mumkin ita bagder wunusu ma Suzaan   abeth, can you converse with Su-
   be Arabi?   zanne in Arabic?'

E: Ya Suzaan, ita indu kam sena fi   'Suzanne, how many years have
   Januub Sudaan ini?   you had in South Sudan?'

S: Hidaasher sena. Zowijuu ana ma   'Eleven years. I am married to a
   zol Januub Sudaani. Ya Elizabeth,   South Sudanese. Elizabeth, do you
   ita gi deresu fi Januub Sudaan ini?   teach in South Sudan here?'

E: Ai, ana gi deresu Ingliizi fi meder-   'Yes, I am teaching English in the
   eesa ta banaat.   girls' school.'

M: Shukran, itakum gi wunusu Arabi   'Thank you. You converse well in
   kweis.   Arabic.'

Kelimaat ziada al der arufu

1. The above classroom vocabulary should help students to use only Arabic in the classroom, so the teacher should use solely Arabic as much as
   possible.

2. Practice questions and answers with *kef* 'how'.

   Ita num kef?
   Ita arifu Arabi kef?
   Ita zekiru deris de kef?
   Ita wunusu be Acholi kef?
   Ita zowijuu ma Januub Sudaani kef?
   Ita afamu zol Ameeriki kef?

3. *Deris ta umbaari de* 'this lesson of yesterday' illustrates that *de* 'this'
   always occurs at the end of a noun phrase, however long, though it
   occurs at the beginning of a noun phrase in English. Also note that its
   specificity may be translated without the word 'this' in some cases,
   e.g., 'yesterday's lesson'; but *de* is needed in Juba Arabic to give that
   specificity.

4. Notice that in *afamu kweis kelima de* 'understand well this word', the
   adverb precedes the object. This is the preferred order: *Ita afamu kweis
   kalaam de?*

5. *Kan ta asma* is a slight abbreviation of *kan ita asma* 'if you hear'. Either
   form is a polite term like 'please'.

6. *Bagder,* like *mumkin,* can be translated 'can'. However, it carries the sense of strength, skill, or knowledge to do something, whereas *mumkin* carries the more general sense of possibility. Practice the following questions with *mumkin* and *bagder,* according to the example shown. Then, answer the following questions:

Mumkin ita bagder katibu waraga fi sobuura?
Mumkin huwo bagder sala arabiiya?
Mumkin ita bagder deresu Arabi?
Mumkin humon bagder wunusu be Ingliizi?

The answers could be either *Ai, mumkin* or *Ai, ana bagder,* or their negations. Practice changing statements into questions with *mumkin* and *bagder,* according to the example shown. Then, answer the following questions:

Huwo sala makana.	Mumkin huwo bagder sala makana?

Biniiya/banaat sala arabiiya.
Katib sala arabiiya.
Itakum fata bab dak.
Ita wunusu be Ingliizi fi medereesa ta banaat?
Humon zekiru deris.
Humon zekiru nimira ta senduuk?
Aniina resemu samaga.
Katib num fi maktab busta.
Biniiya deresu fi medereesa ta makaniiki.

7. *Indu/andu* 'have' is similar to *fi le ana/ita/huwo,* etc. 'there is to me/you/he, etc.'.

Ita indu kam sena fi Januub Sudaan?
Ita indu kam sena fi beled taki?
Ita indu kam shahar fi Juba?
Usbuu indu kam yom?
Shahar indu kam yom?
Sena indu kam yom?
Sa indu kam degiiga?
Yom indu kam sa?
Ita indu kam terebeeza fi bet taki?
Ita indu arabiiya fi bet taki?

8. *Zowijuu* is passive for *zowiju* 'marry'. A man *marries*, but a woman *is married*. This is parallel to the fact that a woman gives birth, *welidu*, but a child is born, *weliduu*.

    James zowiju biniiya Januub Sudaani.
    Suzaan zowijuu ma zol Januub Sudaani.

9. The plural of *biniiya* 'girl' is sometimes *biniyaat,* but is more often *banaat.*

10. *Jawaab* 'letter' also means 'answer'. The verb *jawabu* means 'to reply, answer'. This should be used from now on in reference to questions (*asilaat*) and answers.

    Ita indu asila?   Ai, ita arifu paper be Arabi?
    Ita jawabu kef?   Paper mana to 'waraga'.

Kelimaat

afamu	'understand'
Ameeriki	'American'
andu/indu	'have'
bagder	'can (be able to); know how'
biniiya (*pl* biniyaat/ banaat)	'girl'
del	'these'
Faraansi	'French'
Hindi	'Hindu'
hisa	'class'
indu/andu	'have'
Ingliizi	'English'
jawaab (*pl* jawabaat)	'answer'
jawabu	'reply, answer' *(v)*
kan (i)ta asma	'please, if you will'
mana	'meaning'
muraaja	'review'
num	'sleep'
nus nus	'half and half'
radio	'radio'
sabaa	'morning'
sah	'right, correct'
sobuura	'blackboard'
taliba (*pl* talibaat)	'student'
tani	'again'

u kida	'etc., and so on'
wunusu	'converse'
zekiru	'memorize'
zowiju	'marry'
zowijuu	'married' *(pass)*

Asilaat le temriin

1. Paul u John u Elizabeth u Suzaan kulu humon num kef?
2. Talibaat zekiru deris ta umbaari?
3. Itakum afamu kelima 'safa'?
4. Fi kam safaat fi maktab busta?
5. Seii John arifu kelima *paper* be Arabi?
6. *Paper* mana to shunuu be Arabi?
7. Mumkin ita bagder katibu 'waraga' fi sobuura be Arabi?
8. Seii mudeeris katibu 'waraga' fi sobuura?
9. Seii Elizabeth wunusu ma Paul be Arabi?
10. Mumkin ita bagder wunusu ma sidu dukaan be Arabi?
11. Suzaan indu kam sena fi Januub Sudaan ini?
12. Zowijuu Suzaan ma zol Hindi?
13. Elizabeth gi deresu wen?
14. Elizabeth gi deresu shunuu fi medereesa?
15. Seii Paul yauu gi deresu fi Januub Sudaan ini?
16. Nas Faransiyiin yauu gi wunusu Arabi kweis?
17. Ita arifu wunusu Arabi kweis wala nus nus?
18. Kam kelimaat ita ma afamu fi deris de?
19. Mumkin ita bagder wunusu ma sabii taki be Arabi?
20. Jeraan taki bagder wunusu Arabi ketiir wala Ingliizi ketiir?
21. Talibaat bi katibu fi shunuu?
22. Hisa de hisa shunuu?
23. Ita bagder deresu fi sabaa?
24. U kida mana to shunuu?
25. Kan ta asma mana to shunuu?
26. Huwo jawabu jawaab sah?
27. Fi deris de fi biniiya ta Ingliizi wala ta Ameeriki?
28. Mumkin ita bagder asma Arabi be radio Juba?
29. Ita amulu muraaja le kulu derisiaat del kweis?

Asilaat le muraaja min de-ris nimira sita le ashara

Review questions from lessons 6–10

1. Ita indu kam shahar fi Januub Sudaan?
2. Sikirteer shagaal fi dukaan?
3. Makaniiki gi kasulu afashaat?
4. Mumkin zol selemu jawabaat min senduuk busta kulu yom?
5. Banaat bi derisu Ingliizi fi medereesa?
6. Ita bi safiru ketiir?
7. Itakum bi kelimu Arabi wala itakum bi kelimu Ingliizi ma jeraan?
8. Kubaaya de kweis (kalis) min kubaaya dak?
9. Mumkin ita bagder fata babaat be muftahaat?
10. Jama Juba wenu?
11. Mumkin ita bi wunusu be Arabi?
12. Mariaat fi Januub Sudaan humon bi arifu Ingliizi?
13. Ita zowiju?
14. Ita bi asmau radio fi sabaa?
15. Yal gi geni alabu kweis?
16. Ita akulu bed gidaada umbaari?
17. Itakum zekiru deris ta umbaari?
18. Ita lazim gi geiru zet fi arabiiya kulu usbuu?
19. Itakum bi ashrubu shay ma sukar?

Deris nimira hidaasher   Lesson 11
Ma zol ta makana With the seamstress

Kalaam ma zol ta makana

(A: Amal, G: Gamar)

'Dialogue with a seamstress'

(A: Amal, G: Gamar)

A: Ainu gumaash de. Lon to musu kweis?

'Look at this material. Isn't its color nice?'

G: Kweis. Ita biyuu min wen?

'Nice. Where did you buy it?'

A: Bitaa uma Zenab. Huwo biyuu le ana gumaash de u gumaash dak tegiil min Masir.

'It belongs to Zeinab's mother. She bought me this material and that thick material in Egypt.'

G: Ita gi keitu ketiir?

'Do you sew a lot?'

A: Ai, ana biyuu makana gediim de min gabulu arba sena u ana gi keitu gumashaat ta banaat u ta yal sukeriin.

'Yes, I bought this old machine over four years ago and I sew dresses and children's clothes.'

G: Ita yauu keitu gemiis kebiir de?

'Did you yourself sew this big shirt?'

A: La', de min suk. Ana ma bi keitu gemisiyaat u bantolonaat, bes gumashaat ta mariyaat u ta yal sukeriin.

'No, that's from the market. I don't sew shirts and trousers, only women's and children's clothes.'

G: Ita gi geni keitu shunuu hasi de?

'What are you sewing now?'

A: Fustaan de tawiil.

'This long dress.'

G: Fustaan de ta munuu?

'Who does this dress belong to?'

A: De bitaa Sara. Ita bagder keitu?

'It belongs to Sarah. Do you sew?'

G: Ana ma bagder keitu gumashaat, lakiin ana bi resimu suraat.

'I don't know how to sew clothes, but I embroider pictures.'

71

A: Ita shatir. Ana ma bagder bi resimu   'You are clever. I can't embroider
ta kulu kulu. Resim to sab.   at all.' 'Embroidery is difficult.'
G: Ma sab, sahil. Kayaata sab.   'It's not hard, it's easy. Sewing is
                                          hard.'
A: Mumkin ita amulu le ana sura   'Would you make me a nice picture
kweis u ana bi keitu le ita fustaan?   and I will sew a dress for you?'
G: Kweis, kalaas, aniina rudu.   'Good, it's agreed.'

Kelimaat ziada al der arufu

1. *Musu kweis?* (or *Muze kweis?*) 'Isn't it good?' implies the response *Ai,
   kweis* 'Yes, it's good'; whereas *Lon to ma kweis?* 'Is that color not good?'
   implies the opposite response, *Ai, ma kweis* 'Yes, it's not good'. *Lon to
   kweis?* is neutral, not implying good or bad, though the intonation or
   facial expression could imply one or the other. Practice answering the
   following questions:

   Rajil dak musu kweis? (or ma kweis?)
   Biniiya dak...
   Bet de...
   Shay de...
   Fustaan dak...
   Gumaash dak...
   Gemiis to...
   Bantaloon taki
   Kayaata Amal...
   Resim Gamar...
   Makana Amal...

Next, practice with other adjectives, e.g., *musu jediid* 'not new'; *musu gediim* 'not old'; *musu jahiz* 'not ready'; *musu kafiif* 'not light'. Other adjectives
you can use: *bataal, geriib, sukeer, kebiir, tawiil, tegiil.*

2. The teacher can give any noun and adjective combination. The student
   should repeat the phrase, then respond with the plural. Adjectives are
   not consistently puralized with plural nouns; but when they are, the
   adjective plural ending is always *iin*. For example:

   fustaan tawiil   →   fustanaat tawiliin
   fustaan gediim
   gumaash kafiif
   gemiis kweis
   haja ketiir

jalabiiya bataal
jena sukeer
gufa tegiil
bantoloon jediid
arabiiya geriib
kibda jahiz
degiig sukeer
sabuun tawiil
shurba kebiir

3. *Biyuu* can mean either 'buy' or 'sell', depending on the context. Sometimes the preposition *min* or *le* indicates the difference, e.g., *Ita biyuu makana de min munuu?* 'From whom did you buy this machine?' or *Munuu biyuu makana de le ita?* 'Who sold this machine to you?'

4. *Bitaa* 'belong to' seems to be completely interchangeable with *ta*. Both are used either with nouns or with the question word *munuu* 'who/ whom'? All of the possessive pronouns can be used with or without *bi*. However, the *bitaa* form seems more common in questions. Practice the following questions and answers:

Tabe de bitaa biniiya dak?
    La', tabe de ma bitaa biniiya dak.
    La', tabe de ma bitaa biniiya dak; de bitaa abuu tai.
    La', tabe de bitaai.
Muftaa de bitaa munuu?
Arabiiya de bitaa welid Phillip?
Sobuura de bitaa medereesa?
Kursi de bitaa abuu Sara?
Galam de bitaa sidu dukaan?

5. For further practice with *munuu* 'who?', repeat the questions below and give appropriate answers:

Munuu deru moya?
Munuu bagder keitu fustaan?
Munuu biyuu makana gediim?
Gumaash tegil bitaa munuu?
Gamar wunusu ma munuu?
John biyuu kudruwaat le munuu?
Munuu afamu kweis deris de?
Munuu gi geni fi bet de?

6. *Yauu* is a specifier as in *yauu de* 'this one here'. When it follows a pronoun, it can be translated as a reflexive, e.g., *ita yauu* 'you yourself', *huwo yauu* 'he himself/she herself'.

7. For further practice with nouns and adjectives, repeat the singular sentence, then give the plural without looking:

Bas gediim wagifu gidaam suk.	Basiyaat gedimiin wagifu gidaam suk.
Rajil tawiil ruwa bad asha.	Rujaliin tawiliin ruwa bad asha.
Kadaam ayaan gi geni ishtaagal.	Kadamaat ayaniin gi geni ishtaagal.
Ana biyuu senduuk kweis min suk.	Aniina biyuu sendukaat kweisiin min suk (sukaat).
Ana resimu sura kebiir le welid.	Aniina resimu suraat kebiriin le awlaad.
Jibu gemiis tegiil dak.	Jibu gemisiyaat tegiliin dak.
Ana deru jalabiiya jahiz de.	Aniina deriin jalabiyaat jahiziin de.

8. Study and practice the differences between the following forms. The first is a noun phrase but can also be a stative sentence. The following three are all stative sentences using *de*.

deris sab	'a hard lesson/the lesson is hard'
deris de sab	'this lesson is hard'
de deris sab	'this is a hard lesson'
de deris al sab de	'this is the hard lesson'

Practice all three uses of *de* with each of the following phrases:

kayaata sab
kis fadi
makana gediim
muwaazif shatir
sikirteer kweis
terebeeza tegiil
gufa kafiif

9. Words for 'work' are *shokol* 'work' *(n)*, *shagaal* 'worker' *(n)*, *ishtaagal* 'work' *(v)*, and *takalu* (verb used in some country dialects).

Kelimaat

abuu	'father'
bantoloon (*pl* bantalonaat)	'pants, trousers'
besiit	'easy'; cf. *sahil*
biyuu	'buy, sell'
fustaan (*pl* fustanaat)	'dress'
gabulu	'over'
gediim	'old'
gemiis (*pl* gemiisiyaat)	'shirt'
gumaash (*pl* gumashaat)	'cloth, material, clothes'
ishtaagal	'work' *(v)*
jahiz	'ready, made'
jalabiiya	'jalabiya'
jediid	'new'
kafiif	'light' (weight)
kayaata	'sewing'
keitu	'sew'
kudru/kudra (*pl* kudruwaat/kudrawaat)	'leafy green vegetable'
kursi (*pl* kursiyaat)	'chair'
lon (*pl* lonaat)	'color'
ma kweis	'not good (bad)'
makana	'machine, sewing machine'
Masir	'Egypt'
munuu	'who(m)?'
musu/muze	'not'
musu/muze kweis	'isn't it good?'
resim	'embroidery'
resimu	'draw, embroider'
rudu	'we've agreed'
sab/saab	'difficult, hard'
sahil	'easy'; cf. *besiit*
sukeer	'small'
sura (*pl* suraat)	'picture'
takalu	'work' *(v)*
tawiil (*pl* tuwaliin)	'long, tall'
tegiil	'heavy, thick'
yauu	'self' *(after pro)*
yauu de	'this one here'

Deris nimira itnaasher Dowriiya

Lesson 12
An outing

Kalaam ta ziyaara
(P: Peter, N: nas min kawajaat)

'Dialogue about an outing'
(P: Peter, N: 'group of foreigners')

P: Salaam takum.
N: Ahlen.
P: Itakum gi ruwa le wen?
N: Aniina gi ruwa le Rajaaf.
P: Itakum gi ruwa amulu shunuu hinaak?
N: Aniina gi ruwa sowru bahar u jebel Rajaaf.
P: Itakum ma gi ruwa le jeziira? Jeziira mahaal kweis.
N: Aniina ma arifu teriig.
P: Mumkin itakum bi arkabu murkab.
N: Fi shunuu fi jeziira?
P: Fi jinenaat ketiriin. Fi kudruwaat u fawaaki: lemuun u manga u bordokaal u kida. Jemiil kalis.

N: Mumkin aniina bi dowru fi jineena?

'Hello (everyone).'
'Welcome.'
'Where are you going?'
'We are going to Rejaf.'
'What are you going to do there?'
'We are going to take pictures of the river and Rejaf hill.'
'Are you not going to the island? The island is a nice place.'
'We don't know the way.'
'You can take a boat.'

'What is there on the island?'
'There are lots of gardens. There are vegetables and fruit trees: limes, mangos, oranges, etc. It is beautiful.'
'Can we go for a walk in the gardens?'

77

P: Ai, mumkin itakum bi dowru fi kulu juwa jeziira. Lakiin mata sowru kubri wala nas gi hamim fi bahar.

'Yes, you can walk about the whole island. However, don't take pictures of the bridge or people bathing in the river.'

N: Kweis, shukran le ita.

'Okay, thank you.'

P: Afwan, ma salaam takum.

'You're welcome, goodbye.'

Kelimaat ziada al der arufu

1. Taking pictures of bridges, like military installations, is forbidden. However, the people of South Sudan are also sensitive about photographs which might be taken without permission, and especially of people bathing. A number of foreigners have lost their cameras and a lot of time at the police station.

2. Practice pluralizing nouns and adjectives. Repeat a singular phrase after the teacher, then give the plural:

mudeeris shatir	muderisiin shatiriin	'smart teacher(s)'
biniiya helu	banaat heluiin	'pretty girl(s)'
sawaag ayaan	sawagiin ayaniin	
zol kweis	nas kweisiin	
welid sukeer	awlaad sukeriin	
rajil kebiir	rujaliin kebiriin	
jena jogoot	yal jogotiin	'thin'
mara semiin	mariyaat seminiin	'fat'
def tawiil	diyuuf tawiliin	
kadaam guseer	kadamiin guseriin	'short'
sura kweis	suraat kweisiin	
jeziira jemiil	jeziraat jemiliin	'beautiful'
gemiis kafiif	gemisiaat kafifiin	
fustaan tawiil	fustanaat tawiliin	
muftaa jediid	muftahaat jedidiin	
senduuk tegiil	sendukaat tegiliin	
bab kebiir	babaat kebiriin	

3. Practice substituting nouns and adjectives into the three different sentences below (1, 2, and 3). Noun list (a) goes with sentence (1); noun list (b) with sentence (2); and either noun list (a) or (b) goes with sentence (3). The adjective list goes with all three sentences.

(1) Ana biyuu galam jediid min dukaan.
(2) Welid sukeer biyuu laham min suk.
(3) De deris (al) sab; de derisiaat (al) sabiin.

Nouns (a)	Nouns (b)	Adjectives
kis	welid	tawiil
bantoloon	biniiya	guseer
kubaaya	mara	kebiir
terebeeza	rajil	sukeer
zerif	sawaag	helu
jawaab	katib	kweis
batariiya	kadaam	jahiz
kursi	mudeeris	
radio		
senduuk		

Kelimaat

bordokaal	'orange'
dowriiya	'walk' *(n)*
dowru	'walk' *(v)*
fawaaki	'fruit trees'
guseer	'short'
hamim	'bathe'
helu	'sweet, pretty'
hinaak	'there'
jebel	'hill, mountain'
jemiil	'beautiful, pretty'
jeziira (*pl* jeziraat)	'island'
jineena (*pl* jinenaat)	'garden'
jogoot	'thin, skinny'
juwa	'inside'
kubri	'bridge'
lemuun	'lime(s)'
murkab	'boat'
nas (*sg* zol)	'people'
semiin	'fat'
sowru	'take pictures'
tani	'again'
ziyaara	'visit, outing'

Asilaat le temriin

1. Nas munuu ruwa le ziyaara, u wen?
2. Nas min kawajaat humon ruwa amulu shunuu fi Rejaaf?
3. Humon sowru shunuu u shunuu?
4. Nas munuu ma arifu teriig ta jeziira?

5. Fi shunuu kweis fi jeziira?
6. Munuu kelimu, "Matakum sowru kubri"?
7. Kan ita deru ruwa le jeziira, ita bi ruwa be shunuu?
8. Murkab mana to shunuu be Ingliizi?
9. Kubri kebiir fi Juba kubri shunuu?
10. Ita gi hamim fi bet wala fi bahar?
11. Mahaal jemiil kalis fi Juba shunuu?
12. Biniiya helu wala jemiil?
13. Ita tawiil wala guseer?
14. Ita gi biyuu kudruwaat taki wen?
15. Humon gi jibu kudruwaat u fawaaki min wen?
16. Ita akulu bordokaal fi Januub Sudaan ini?
17. Manga ketiir kalis fi jeziira?
18. Fawaaki fi Januub Sudaan ini helu kalis min fawaaki ta beled takum?
19. Ita ainu Rejaaf yom tani wala la'?
20. Itakum ruwa le jeziira yom wahid u be shunuu?
21. Dowriiya le Jebel Rejaaf musu kweis?
22. Fi sabaa ita dowru wen?
23. Nas semiin akulu fawaaki ketiir, muze sah?
24. Murkab ruwa tehet kubri wala gabulu kubri?
25. Sowru munuu jemiil kalis?
26. Ita deru ashrubu lemuun ma bun?
27. Munuu jogoot kalis min mudeeris?
28. Nas Ameeriki bi ziyaara miteen?
29. Ita arifu takalu be makana kayaata?
30. Ita kan takalu fi jineena?

Deris nimira talataasher
Ma ahal ta bet

Lesson 13
With a family

Kalaam ma ahal ta bet
(P: Peter, J: Jafar)

'Dialogue with a family'
(P: Peter, J: Jafar)

P: Salaam taki.
'Peace to you.'

J: Ahlen.
'Welcome.'

P: Itakum kweisiin?
'Are all of you well?'

J: Kweisiin, ma bataliin. Gisim kef?
'Fine, not bad. How is your health?'

P: Kweis, ma bataal. Ita woduru wen?
Ita gi geni zaman de wen?
'Fine, not bad. Where have you been?
Where have you been all this time?'

J: Ana fi zaman tawiil ma ainu ita.
Ita gi geni zaman de wen?
'I didn't see you for a long time.
Where have you been all this
time?'

P: Abuu taki kef? Huwo kweis?
'How is your father? Well, I hope.'

J: Ai, huwo kweis.
'Yes, he's fine.'

P: Kabar ta akuu taki kef?
'What's the news of your brother?'

J: Huwo kweis kalis. Huwo zowiju fi
sena de.
'He is very well. He got married
this year.'

P: Zowiju biniiya ta munuu?
'Whose daughter did he marry?'

J: Huwo zowiju biniiya ta Biajo.
Abuu taki kweis?
'He married Biajo's daughter. Is
your father well?'

P: Ai, huwo kweis, lakiin abuuba tai
ayaan.
'Yes, he's well, but my grandmother is ill.'

J: Kafaara, huwo bi kun kweis.
'I hope she will be well soon.'

P: Kan Rabuuna saaidu huwo.
'Thank you—if God helps her.'

J: Huwo ayaan be shunuu?
'What illness does she have?'

P: Huwo ayaan be waja dahar.
'She's got a pain in her back.'

81

J: Kelii Rabuuna saaidu huwo.   'May the Lord help her.'
P: Okot taki kef? Ana asma huwo   'How is your sister? I heard that
   kan ayaan.   she was sick.'
J: Ai, huwo kan ayaan, lakiin huwo   'Yes, she was sick but she got well.'
   biga kweis.

Kelimaat ziada al der arufu

1. Uncles and aunts must be distinguished as to whether they are related
    on the father's side or the mother's side: *akuu abuu tai* 'my father's
    brother' and *okot abuu tai* 'my father's sister' or *kal tai* 'my mother's
    brother' and *kalti tai* 'my mother's sister'.

2. Cousins, likewise, are the sons and daughters of these uncles and aunts,
    e.g., *welid ta kalti tai* 'son of my mother's sister'.

3. Grandparents of both sides are called *jidi* 'grandfather' and *abuuba*
    'grandmother'.

4. In South Sudan, it is not allowed to marry one's cousin.

5. The order of one kind of English noun phrase is: possessor/adjective/
    noun, e.g., 'my small boy'. But in Arabic the order is usually noun/pos-
    sessor/adjective, e.g., *welid tai sukeer*. Practice making noun phrases
    with the following words (given below in wrong order for more mean-
    ingful practice):

tai	sukeer	welid
taki	kebiir	abuu
to	tawiil	akuu
taniina	jogoot	okot
takum	semiin	kal
tomon	ayaan	kalti
	guseer	mudeeris
	akuu	abuu
	okot	abuu

6. Answer the following questions:

    Okot taki kef?
    Mudeeris takum safiru umbaari?
    Okot taki gi deresu shunuu?
    Gufa to wenu?

Ita woduru sa taki?
Welid taniina ayaan be shunuu?
Munuu sala arabiiya taki?
Kadaam to gi kasulu gumashaat?
Ita rasulu jawaab le uma taki?
Medereesa to fi fi Juba wala fi Toriit?
Def takum gi ashrubu shay?
Fi zol tomon ayaan fi Yei?

7. Practice family nouns:

Abuuba tai (huwo) ayaan be waja dahar.
Akuu taniina (huwo) ja min Yei.
Kal tai (huwo) zowiju fi sena de.
Okot taki (huwo) gi geni wen?
Jidi tomon (huwo) mutu umbaari?
Okot abuu takum (huwo) mudeeris fi Toriit.

8. *Indu* 'have' has three optional forms for *I, we,* and *they*.

ana indu/indi
ita indu
huwo indu
aniina indu/indana
itakum indu
humon indu/indum

9. Practice making statements like the following:

Ana asma ita kan ayaan.   'I heard that you were sick.'

Kelimaat

abuuba	'grandmother'
ahal	'family'
akuu	'brother'
akuu abuu	'uncle (father's brother)'
bi kun	'will be'
biga	'became, got to be'
dahar/daar	'back'
gisim	'body, health'
indana/indu	'we have' (ed.)
indi/indu	'I have' (ed.)

indum/indu	'they have' (ed.)
jidi	'grandfather'
kabar (*pl* akbar)	'news'
kafaara	'sympathy'
kal	'uncle (mother's brother)'
kalti	'aunt (mother's sister)'
mutu	'die, death'
okot/ukut (*pl* ikwaat)	'sister'
okot abuu	'aunt (father's sister)'
talataasher	'thirteen'
Toriit	'Torit'
waja	'pain, ache'
woduru	'be'
wokit	'period of time'
zaman	'period of time'

Asilaat le temriin

1. Ita kweis?
2. Ahal taki kef, humon kweisiin?
3. Gisim taki kef?
4. Ita fi wokit de wen?
5. Ahal taki fi bet, kef humon?
6. Abuuba tomon kef?
7. Kabar ta nas hasi de kef?
8. Kabar ta nas Malakal kef?
9. Ita zowiju fi sena de?
10. Yal taki fi beled takum?
11. Itakum fi Juba gi geni kef?
12. Akuu taki hasi de fi Januub Sudaan fi?
13. Kal taki fi wala mafi?
14. Okot abuu taki zowijuu?
15. Fi shunuu gi waja fi gisim taki hasi de?
16. Fi wahid min akwaana taki gi geni fi Juba ini?
17. Fi zol tomon ayaan ini?
18. Munuu ayaan be waja dahar?
19. Jidi taki kef hasi de?
20. Kal tomon ruwa le wen?

Deris nimira arbataasher　　Lesson 14
Rihla le Nimule　　　　　A trip to Nimule

Kalaam ta rihla le Nimule

(P: Paul, M: Moses, E: Elizabeth)

'Dialogue about a trip to Nimule'

(P: Paul, M: Moses, E: Elizabeth)

P: Aniina rija min Nimule awal umbaari.

'We returned from Nimule the day before yesterday.'

M: Nimule kef?

'How was Nimule?'

P: Nimule kweis kalis.

'Nimule was very beautiful.'

E: Aniina ainu haywanaat ketiir fi teriig ben Juba u Nimule, zaraaf u filaat u guruud.

'We saw a lot of animals on the road between Juba and Nimule: giraffes, elephants, monkeys.'

M: Itakum ma kafu min haywanaat del?

'Weren't you afraid of these animals?'

P: La', aniina kan ma nas ta beled u aniina ma nezil min arabiiya.

'No, we were with local people and didn't get out of the car.'

M: Akuu abuu tai fi Nimule kelimu nas gi durubu filaat u gi shilu sununaat tomon ashaan aj.

'My uncle in Nimule said that people are hunting the elephants and are taking their tusks for the ivory.'

E: Sah, fi nas gi durubu, lakiin abaau le zol al ma indu roksa.

'That's true; there are people hunting but it's forbidden without a license.'

M: Itakum ligoo akuu abuu tai? Huwo ishtaagal fi maktab busta.

'Did you meet my uncle? He works in the post office.'

P: Ai, dor wahid bes. Huwo kweis u kamaan kweisiin yal to.

'Yes, just once. He's well and his children are also well.'

85

Kelimaat ziada al der arufu

1. *Kan* 'was/were' does not occur in the present tense.

    Aniina kan ma nas ta beled.   'We were with the local people.'
    Aniina ma nas ta beled.   'We are with the local people.'

2. Learn numbers 20–100. It would be helpful for the teacher to drill the
    students with flashcards.

    20 ishriin
    21 wahid u ishriin
    22 itiniin u ishriin
        etc.
    30 teletiin
    40 arbeyiin
    50 kamsiin
    60 sitiin
    70 sebeyiin
    80 tamaniin
    90 tiseyiin
    100 miya

3. Practice indirect speech. The teacher should give a speech-verb and
    have the student complete the sentence. Note that relationship terms
    must have a possessor, e.g., *sabii to* 'his friend', *okot to* 'his sister'.

    Huwo   kelimu   nas gi durubu filaat.
    Huwo   asmau   nas ta beled ma kafu.
    Huwo   asmau   akuu sabii tai zowiju fi sena de.
    Huwo   zekiru   abuuba to ayaan be waja dahar.
    Huwo   jawabu   okot to kan ayaan.
    Huwo   asalu   akuu abuu to gi ishtaagal fi Nimule.
    Huwo   asalu   fi haywanaat ketiir ben Juba u Nimule.

    In an indirect quotation, second and third person subjects are expressed
as follows:

    John kelimu le huwo kelii (huwo) wodii le ana guruush.
    'John told him to (let him) give me money.'
    John kelimu le humon kelii (humon) ruwa le suk biyuu laham.
    John kelimu le ita kelii ita wodii le ana guruush.
    John kelimu le itakum kelii itakum amulu akil ta gada.

(See lesson 22 for first person subjects.)

4. Notice the preposition *min* in *rija min* 'return from', *kafu min* 'afraid of', and *nenzil min* 'get down from'.

5. Practice expanding the following sentences as the teacher supplies additional words. Sometimes you must add additional words like prepositions in order for the sentence to make sense.

    Cue words
	Aniina ainu haywanaat.
ketiir	Aniina ainu haywanaat ketiir.
teriig	Aniina ainu haywanaat ketiir fi teriig.
kweis	Aniina ainu haywanaat ketiir fi teriig kweis.
Juba u Nimule	Aniina ainu haywanaat ketiir fi teriig kweis ben Juba u Nimule
	Itakum kafu?
ma	Itakum ma kafu?
haywanaat	Itakum ma kafu min haywanaat?
del	Itakum ma kafu min haywanaat del?
	Itakum ligoo abuu tai?
Nimule	Itakum ligoo abuu tai fi Nimule?
ishtaagal	Itakum ligoo abuu tai fi Nimule gi ishtaagal?
maktab busta	Itakum ligoo abuu tai fi Nimule gi ishtaagal fi maktab busta?
Umbaari	(Umbaari) itakum ligoo abuu tai fi Nimule gi ishtaagal fi maktab busta (umbaari)?

6. Practice completing the following phrases as shown in the first example:

    Durubu fil   abaau le zol al ma indu roksa.
    Shilu sununaat tomon
    Sowru kubri
    Sowru nas gi hamim
    Sugu arabiiya
    Biyuu laham fi suk
    Biyuu sukar fi dukaan

7. One can say either *dor wahid* or *wahid dor* 'once, one time, one turn'; however, the former is more common. On the other hand, other numbers are more commonly stated in the latter order, e.g., *itiniin dor* 'twice, two times'.

Kelimaat

abaau	'forbidden to'
aj	'ivory'
arbataasher	'fourteen'
arbeyiin	'forty'
asala	'question' *(v)*
ashaan	'for'
awal	'first, before'
awal umbaari	'day before yesterday'
ben	'between'
dor	'time, turn'
dor wahid/wahid dor	'once, one time, one turn'
durubu	'hunt, shoot'
fil (*pl* filaat)	'elephant'
girid (*pl* guruud)	'monkey'
haywaan (*pl* haywanaat)	'animal'
itiniin dor	'twice'
kafu (min)	'afraid of'
kamsiin	'fifty'
ligoo	'meet'
miya	'one hundred'
nenzil/nezil	'get down'
rihla	'outing'
roksa/ruksa	'license'
sabii	'friend'
sebeyiin	'seventy'
shilu	'take'
sitiin	'sixty'
sugu	'drive'
sunuun (*pl* sununaat)	'tusk'
tamaniin	'eighty'
teletiin	'thirty'
tiseyiin	'ninety'
wahid dor/dor wahid	'once, one time, one turn'
zaraaf	'giraffe'

Asilaat le temriin

1. Ita rija min Nimule awal umbaari?
2. Nimule kef?
3. Ita ainu haywanaat ketiir fi Juba ini?
4. Nas munuu kafu min haywanaat?

5. Itakum gi kafu min haywaan hasi de?
6. Nas munuu kan ma nas ta beled?
7. Nas munuu ma nenzil min arabiiya?
8. Seii ita durubu haywaan yom wahid?
9. Ita seii, ligoo guruush fi teriig ta Juba?
10. Munuu ligoo akuu abuu to fi Nimule?
11. Akuu abuu to shagaal shunuu?
12. Ita ruwa fi Nimule kam dor?
13. Yal ta munuu humon kweisiin?
14. Ita ainu Nimule yom wahid?
15. Humon indu bet fi Juba ini?
16. Seii ita ruwa yom wahid rihla fi Juba?
17. Zaman ita ruwa umbaari fi suk ma munuu?
18. Ita ainu fil fi Juba?
19. Seii itakum ainu jama ta Juba?
20. Fi shunuu yatuu haywanaat fi Juba?

Deris nimira kamastaasher   Lesson 15
Shokol fi bet   Housework

Kalaam ta shokol fi bet

(M: mara, K: kadaam)

M: Ya Kukuu

K: Ai.

M: Nedifu oda juluus u oda num u kasulu esmiinti ta juwa kweis.

K: Kweis lazim. U ana bi kasulu terebezaat u kursiyaat?

M: Ai, kasulu terebezaat u kursiyaat kamaan. Kan fi turaab ketiir umbaari. Badeen kasulu gumashaat del.

K: Yom itniini al fat ma fi sabuun.

M: Fi hasi de. Mahajuub jibu kortoon kebiir min dukaan. Yauu de.

K: Mokwa wenu?

M: Ainu fi dolaab fi juwa motbak.

K: Ai, fi.

M: Kweis. Ita bi safiru bukra?

K: Ai. Mumkin ana bi shilu guruush tai aleela?

'Dialogue about housework'

(M: 'woman', K: 'house helper')

'Kookoo.'

'Here.'

'Clean the living room and the bedroom and wash the floors well.'

'Okay. Do I need to clean the tables and the chairs?'

'Yes, clean the tables and the chairs too. It was very dusty yesterday. And then wash these clothes.'

'On Monday there wasn't soap.'

'There is now. Mahjoub brought a large box from the shop. Here it is!'

'Where's the iron?'

'Look in the cupboard in the kitchen.'

'Yes, it's here.'

'Good. Are you going away tomorrow?'

'Yes. May I take my money today?'

M: Mumkin, bad gada. Ana gi ruwa le
   suk. Mata fatau shubakaat ashaan
   sukun.
K: Kweis.

'Yes, after dinner. I am going to
market. Don't open the windows
because it is hot.'
'Okay.'

Kelimaat ziada al der arufu

1. The past tense of *fi* 'there is' is either *kan fin* or *fi kan*. The past negative
   is *ma fi kan* 'there wasn't/weren't'.

2. The Mahjoub referred to in the dialogue is presumed to be the woman's
   husband. South Sudanese generally refer to their husbands by name in
   speaking to house workers or other adults. Children often refer to their
   parents by name also. With the exception of a few families, South Sudanese do not have a surname or family name in the European sense.
   Each person has a given name and after it adds the name of his or
   her father and then grandfather in order to distinguish himself/herself
   from other individuals with the same given name, e.g., Mohammed
   Hassan Ali or Monica Hassan Ali.

3. The imperative is used for giving orders. When in English one would
   use 'please' in a polite request—e.g., 'Would you get me a spoon
   please?'—in Arabic one would not normally use 'please' in this sort of
   request. Practice the following singular and plural imperatives by doing the action:

   fata bab   fata takum babaat
   gofolu shubaak   gofol takum shubakaat
   resemu sura   (u kida)
   katibu haja be Ingliizi
   dafa le ana kamsiin jinee
   dakulu galam fi kis
   kelim ma mudeeris
   katibu be galam
   jibu arba jinee
   shilu kubaaya min terebeeza

4. Practice negative imperatives:

   singular: mata fata bab
   plural: matakum fata bab/babaat

The teacher may give imperatives and the students negate them.

5. Review the numbers 20–100 from lesson 14. Then memorize the numbers below:

100	miya
101	miya u wahid
125	miya (u) kamsa u ishriin
200	miteen
300	tultomiiya
400	orbomiiya
500	komsomiiya
600	sutumiiya
700	subumiiya
800	tumonmiiya
900	tusomiiya
1000	alf
2000	itiniin alf
1,000,000	milyoon

Kelimaat

afeendi (*pl* afeendiyaat)	'official' *(n)*
alf/alaf	'one thousand'
barid	'cold'
dolaab	'cupboard'
esmiinti	'cement floor'
fat	'last, previous'
fogo	'in it'
juwa	'house, inside place'
kamastaasher	'fifteen'
kasuru	'broken (not glass)'
komsomiiya	'five hundred'
kortoon	'cardboard box'
le	'why?'; cf. *shunuu*
milyoon	'one million'
miteen	'two hundred'
mokwa	'iron, ironing'
motbak	'kitchen'
nedifu	'clean'
oda num	'bedroom'
orbomiiya	'four hundred'
shubaak (*pl* shubakaat)	'window'
shunuu	'why?'; cf. *le*
subumiiya	'seven hundred'

sukun	'hot'
sutumiiya	'six hundred'
tultomiiya	'three hundred'
tumonmiiya/ tumunumiiya	'eight hundred'
turaab	'dust, dirt'
tusomiiya	'nine hundred'
yom itniini	'Monday'

Asilaat le temriin

1. Bet taki fi fogo oda juluus?
2. Munuu bi nedifu oda juluus u oda num fi bet taki?
3. Ita bi nedifu bet taki kef? U be shunuu?
4. Munuu bi kasulu gumashaat taki?
5. Ita bi kasulu gumashaat kef? Be makana? Be sabuun shunuu?
6. Kan fi turaab ketiir fi oda num taki, ita bi num kweis?
7. Kan fi turaab ketiir fi akil, ita bi akulu kweis?
8. Yom itniini al fat ita kan wen? Ita amulu shunuu?
9. Ita biyuu sabuun kef? Be kortoon kebiir?
10. Ita mokwa be mokwa barid wala be mokwa sukun?
11. Fi shunuu fi dolaab fi juwa motbak?
12. Kukuu munuu? Kukuu bi safiru miteen?
13. Kukuu deru shilu shunuu?
14. Mara deru dafau guruush miteen?
15. Mara deru ruwa le wen awal?
16. Mara kelimu le Kukuu mata amulu shunuu? Le?
17. Fi oda de fi kam shubakaat? Fi bet de?
18. Kulu usbuu ita bi nedifu bet u bi kasulu gumashaat taki?
19. Kulu usbuu ita bi mokwa gemiis wala fustaan taki?
20. Shunuu yauu kweis le ita: kasulu gumashaat wala mokwa gumashaat?
21. Kan ma fi moya, ita bi kasulu gumashaat kef?
22. Kan ma fi akil fi bet, ita bi akulu gada kef? Wen?
23. Kan oda sukun, ita bi gofulu shubakaat?
24. Mahajuub munuu?
25. Fi bet taki fi fogo esmiinti?
26. Ita akulu shunuu fi gada aleela?
27. Bad gada ita bi amulu shunuu?
28. Be itniin jinee mumkin ita bi biyuu haja?
29. Terebezaat u kursiyaat gi geni fi oda shunuu?

Asilaat le muraaja min deris nimira hidaasher le kamastaasher

Review questions from lessons 11–15

1. Ita bi jibu galam u waraga le hisa Arabi?
2. Lazim kadaam nedifu turaab fi bet fi Juba?
3. Munuu bi kasulu afashaat fi bet takum?
4. Fi filaat u guruud fi beled taki?
5. Ita ainu zaraaf fi Nimule?
6. Akuu Jafar zowiju munuu?
7. Januub Sudaniin bi derisu Arabi wala bi derisu Ingliizi fi medereesa?
8. Fustaan taki tawiil wala guseer?
9. Fi sena fi kam yom: 365 wala 366?
10. Afendiyaat Januub Sudaniin bi ishtaagal fi Juba fi yom itniini?
11. Mudeeris takum gi asmau akbar min radio Juba?
12. Ita bi arifu durubu haywanaat?
13. Welid taki sukeer ma num lisa?
14. Yom itniini al fat yom kam fi shahar?
15. Kan fi haja kasuru fi motbak taki awal umbaari?
16. Mudeeris ta Arabi bi katibu fi sobuura?
17. Ita bi dafau kam le kudruwaat fi kulu usbuu?
18. Bordokaal fi Januub Sudaan ini helu?
19. Aniina rija min rihla le Nimule miteen?
20. Ita sowru shunuu fi Juba?
21. Abaau sowru shunuu fi Juba?
22. Ita deru hajaat min aj?
23. Ita deru gumaash jediid wala gumaash gediim?

95

24. Ita deru esh jediid wala esh gediim?
25. Yom sukun ita deru gemiis tegiil?
26. Jebel geriib min Juba jebel shunuu?
27. Ita deru dowru fog jebel de?
28. Yal taki kulu humon shatiriin?
29. Kukuu kelimu huwo bi kasulu shunuu?
30. Mara kelimu le Kukuu kelii huwo ja shilu guruush miteen?

Deris nimira sitaasher Kura gadam

Lesson 16 The football game

Kalaam ta kura gadam
(P: Phillip, K: Kamaal)

'Dialogue about the football game'
(P: Phillip, K: Kamal)

P: Ita ainu mubaraa ben Kator u Malakia fi yom sebit al fat?

'Did you see the match between Kator and Malakia last Saturday?'

K: Ai, ana ainu.

'Yes, I saw it.'

P: Gilibuu nas munuu?

'Which people were defeated?'

K: Malakia gilibu Kator itiniin sifir. Gon nimira itiniin kan gabulu nihaaya mubaraa be itiniin degiiga.

'Malakia defeated Kator 2–0. The second goal came two minutes before the end of the match.'

P: Mubaraa kan kef?

'What sort of match was it?'

K: Kan kida u kida. Fi shot nimira itiniin humon alabu kweis ashaan humon sakanu.

'So-so. They played better in the second half because they had warmed up.'

P: Munuu sejilu itiniin gon de?

'Who scored the two goals?'

K: De jenaa ta yamiin sejilu nimira wahid, wa dib sejilu nimira itiniin.

'It was the right wing who scored the first goal, the center (forward) the second one.'

P: Huwo lahib jediid, muze de?

'He is a new player, isn't he?'

K: Ai, huwo kan kweis kalis.

'Yes, he was excellent.'

P: Usbuu al jay mubaraa ma munuu?

'Who's the match against next week?'

K: Ma Nasir fi dar riyaada.

'Against Nasit at the stadium.'

P: Kalaas kweis. Aniina bi limu hinaak. Ma salaam taki.

'Okay. Let's meet there. Goodbye.'

97

Kelimaat ziada al der arufu

1. Once you know the numbers in Arabic it is easy to learn the names
    of the days of the week and the months, because most of them are
    derived from numbers. Memorize the following list of the days of
    the week:

yom lahad	'Sunday'
yom itniini	'Monday'
yom talaata	'Tuesday'
yom arbaa	'Wednesday'
yom kamiis	'Thursday'
yom juma	'Friday'
yom sebit	'Saturday'

2. The months of the year are usually referred to by their number, e.g.,
    January is *shahar wahid*. As such, January 1 is *yom wahid fi shahar wa-
    hid* or *wahid wahid*. Answer the following questions:

    Aleela yom talaata?
    Bukra shunuu?
    Sena jay kam?/Sena jay sena kam?
    Shahar al fat kan shunuu?
    Weliduu ita fi shahar ashara?
    Umbaari yom kam?
    Aleela yom kam?
    Bukra yom kam?

    Note that a question requiring an answer in numbers always uses *kam*
    'how many' even where one would use 'what' in English, e.g., *Aleela yom
    kam?* 'What day is today?'

3. *Munuu* can be transated 'who?' or 'whom?'. Repeat the following ques-
    tions after the teacher and give appropriate answers:

Gilibuu nas munuu?	'Who was defeated?'
Usbuu jay mubaraa ma munuu?	'With whom is next week's match?'
Munuu sejilu itiniin gon de?	'Who scored the two goals?
Munuu ita saaidu?	'Whom did you help?'
Munuu huwo saaidu?	'Who (he) helped you?'

Bet ta munuu ita ruwa fogo?	'To whose house did you go?'
Bet ta munuu ita ja min fogo?	'From whose house did you come?'
Gidaam bet ta munuu ita wagifu fogo?	'In front of whose house did you stop?'
Le munuu ita ruwa?	'To whom did you go?'

(Note that the 'whose' question requires *fogo*.)

4. The first person singular and plural of the future can be used to express 'let me' or 'let us'. In the dialogue Phillip says: *Aniina bi limu hinaak* 'Let's meet there'.

Kelimaat

al jay	'next, coming'
dar riyaada	'stadium'
dib	'center (football player)'
gadam	'foot'
gilibu	'defeat'
gilibuu	'defeated'
gon	'goal'
jenaa	'wing (player)'
kida u kida	'so-so'
kura	'ball'
lahib	'player'
mubaraa	'match, game'
nihaaya	'end'
sakanu	'warm up'
sebit; yom sebit	'Saturday'
sejilu	'score'
shot	'half (of a football game)'
sifir	'zero'
sitaasher	'sixteen'
yom arbaa	'Wednesday'
yom juma	'Friday'
yom kamiis	'Thursday'
yom lahad	'Sunday'
(yom) sebit	'Saturday'
yom talaata/ salasaa	'Tuesday'

Asilaat le temriin

1. Munuu yauu ainu mubaraa ben Malakia u Kator, u miteen?
2. Kan gilibu nas munuu?
3. Gilibu Kator kam?
4. Mubaraa kan kef?
5. Nas munuu yauu alabu kweis?
6. Munuu yauu sejilu gon nimira wahid?
7. Munuu yauu sejilu gon nimira itiniin, u fi degiiga kam?
8. Munuu yauu kan lahib jediid?
9. Munuu yauu kan alabu kweis kalis fi mubaraa de?
10. Usbuu al jay mubaraa ma munuu?
11. Humon bi alabu wen?
12. Kura gadam kweis kalis le ita wala la'?
13. Ita seii, yom wahid alabu kura gadam?
14. Kura shunuu yauu kweis le ita?
15. Nas ta beled takum gi alabu kura gadam?
16. Munuu kelimu, aniina bi limu fi dar riyaada?
17. Ita indu kura gadam fi bet taki?
18. Ita ainu mubaraa fi Januub Sudaan ini u wen?
19. Ita ainu mubaraa fi beled takum ben nas munuu?
20. Mubaraa ta kura gadam gi alabu kam degiiga?

Deris nimira sabataasher   Lesson 17
Hafla shay   A tea party

Kalaam ta hafla shay   'Dialogue about a tea party'
(S: Samya, F: Fatima, M: Marie)   (S: Samya, F: Fatima, M: Marie)

S: Ya kalti, de sabii tai min Faraansa.   'Aunt, this is my friend from
    Huwo indu sena wahid fi Januub   France. She has been in South Su-
    Sudaan ini. Huwo gi geni geriib   dan one year. She lives near us.'
    ma aniina.

F: Fadal, geni.   'Please sit down.'

S: U de kalti tai, isim to Fatima.   'And this is my aunt, her name is
                                              Fatima.'

F: Isim taki munuu?   'What is your name?'

M: Isim tai Marie.   'My name is Marie.'

F: Kelim tani.   'Pardon me? (lit. Say it again.)'

M: Marie.   'Marie.'

F: Zowijuu ita?   'Are you married?'

M: Ai, rajil tai muhaandis fi sherika ta   'Yes, my husband is an engineer
    Faraansa u Januub Sudaan.   with the Franco-South Sudanese
                                              company.'

F: Ita indu yal?   'Do you have any children?'

M: Ai, talaata, itiniin welid u wahid   'Yes, three. Two boys and one girl.
    biniiya. Ita indu yal kamaan?   Do you have any?'

F: Ai, kamsa. Wahid fi jesh u wahid   'Yes, five. One is in the army, one is
    gi geni ma jidi tai fi Toriit u taniin   living with my grandfather in Torit
    mai ini.   and the others are here with me.'

M: Ita gi ishtaagal shediid. Fi welid gi   'You must be busy. Do you have
    ishtaagal ma ita?   house-help?'

F: La', ana gi ishtaagal baraau, u de   'No, I do my own housework, and
   sab ashaan ana indu shokol bara.   that's hard because I have a job too.'
   (Samya gi jibu shay.)   ('Samya brings tea.')
S: Fadal takum.   'Please drink.'
F: Ashrib! Sukar kweis?   'Drink up! Is the sugar enough?'
M: Shukran. Fi sukar kweis.   'Thank you. There's enough sugar.'

Kelimaat ziada al der arufu

1. In Arabic, ask *Isim taki munuu?*, not *Isim taki shunuu?*

2. Prepositions:

With pronouns:	Other:
ma ana	fog juwa
ma ita	tehet bara
ma huwo	gidaam hawe
ma aniina	wara esh
ma itakum	
ma humon	

Instead of *ma ana* and *le ana,* some people use *mai* and *lei. Gidaam* 'in front of' is sometimes treated as a noun, sometimes as a preposition, i.e., *gidaam tai* or *gidaam ana* 'in front of me'.

The teacher should take any object and place it somewhere in relation to himself/herself or one of the students. For example, the teacher can put a pen in front of a student and ask, "Galam wenu?" The student replies, "Galam fi gidaam tai/ana", and so on. Also the teacher may hold a pen above the table and ask, "Galam fog terebeeza?" The student replies, "Ai, galam fi fogo."

3. *Indu* translates as 'have'. Practice this verb with the following questions and answers:

Ita indu arabiiya?	La', ana ma indu arabiiya.
Ita indu awlaad?	Ai, ana indu awlaad.
Huwo indu radio jediid?	La', huwo indu radio gediim.
Aniina indu makana kayaata?	Ai, aniina indu makana kayaata.
Itakum indu diyuuf aleela?	Ai, aniina indu diyuuf aleela.
Humon indum bet fi Juba?	La', humon indum bet fi Toriit.

4. *Baraau is translated as* 'alone, on one's own'. Below is a set of questions for the teacher to ask the students. The students should reply using *baraau.*

Huwo gi ruwa ma ita?   La', huwo gi ruwa baraau.
Humon gi ruwa ma itakum?
Biniiya bi ishtaagal ma ita?
Ita gi ruwa ma uma taki?
Welid katibu jawaab ma okot to?
Kadamiin bi ishtaagal ma itakum?

Kelimaat

baraau	'alone; on one's own'
Faraansa	'France'
hafla (*pl* haflaat)	'party'
hawe	'around, surrounding'
isim	'name'
jesh	'army'
le ana; lei	'to me'
ma ana; mai	'with me'
ma humon; moom	'with them'
ma huwo; moo	'with him/her/it'
muhaandis	'engineer'
sabataasher	'seventeen'
sherika	'company'

Asilaat le temriin

1. Munuu yauu min Faraansa?
2. Munuu yauu indu sena wahid fi Januub Sudaan?
3. Samya kalti to isim to munuu?
4. Marie rajil to shagaal shunuu?
5. Marie indu kam yal?
6. Munuu yauu indu kamsa yal?
7. Munuu jena bitoo shagaal jesh?
8. Munuu indu shokol bara?
9. Isim taki munuu u isim ta abuu taki munuu?
10. Ita indu kam yal?
11. Ita lisa ma zowiju mara?
12. Ita gi ishtaagal fi bet baraau wala ma zol tani?
13. Ita indu sabii taki isim to munuu?
14. Lisa ita ma indu yal?

15. Ita gi geni fi bet taki baraau?
16. Isim ta uma taki munuu?
17. Ita indu kam okotaat?
18. Munuu yauu weliduu awal fi bet takum?
19. Sabii taki gi ja kulu yom fi bet taki?
20. Uma taki fi fi Januub Sudaan ini wala fi beled takum?

Deris nimira tamantaasher   Lesson 18
Mala form   Filling in a form

Kalaam ta mala form

(K: kawaaja, S: Januub Sudaani)

K: Ya sabii tai, lazim ana bi mala form de, lakiin ana ma arifu agra Arabi. Mumkin ita katibu le ana?

S: Kweis. Isim taki munuu?

K: Wolfgang Behrens.

S: Nimira itiniin: jinis taki shunuu?

K: Almaania.

S: Kweis. Waziifa taki shunuu, yani ita shagaal shokol shunuu?

K: Zol indu fikra fi ziraa.

S: Nimira pasport taki kam?

K: Katibuu ini fi nota u anwaan tai kamaan.

S: Nihaaya, ita ja fi Januub Sudaan ini miteen?

K: Ana ja fi shahar arba, yom teletiin, fi sena de.

S: Kweis, kalaas.

K: Shukran shediid le ita.

'Dialogue about filling in a form'

(K: 'foreigner', S: 'South Sudanese')

'Friend, I have to fill in this form but I can't read Arabic. Could you write for me?'

'Good. What is your name?'

'Wolfgang Behrens.'

'Number 2: What's your nationality?'

'German.'

'Good. What is your occupation, that's to say, your work?'

'Agriculturalist.'

'What's the number of your passport?'

'It's written here in my notebook, and my address too.'

'Lastly, what was the date of your arrival in South Sudan?'

'I arrived on April 30th this year.'

'Fine, that's all.'

'Many thanks.'

Kelimaat ziada al der arufu

1. With the teacher's help, go through both questions you have been asked
    by officials and the questions in the dialogue and provide answers rel-
    evant to yourself. Once you've done this, memorize the answers that go
    along with these questions.

Isim taki munuu?	'What is your name?'
Waziifa taki shunuu?	'What is your occupation?'
Nimira pasport taki kam?	'What is your passport number?'
Jibuu ita fi Januub Sudaan le shunuu?	'Why did you come to South Sudan?'
Ita fi Januub Sudaan ini gi geni wen?	'Where do you stay in South Sudan?'
Anwaan taki shunuu?	'What's your address?'
Ita ja min wen?	'Where do you come from?'
Ita gi ishtaagal ma munaazama shunuu?	'With which organization are you working?'

2. Next, complete the following expansion drill. The purpose of the drill is
    to gain control over longer stretches of speech. The teacher should say the
    sentences below at normal speed with students repeating after the teacher.

    a. Huwo biyuu gumaash jahiz.
        Munuu biyuu gumaash jahiz?
        Okot tai sukeer biyuu gumaash jahiz.
        Okot taki sukeer biyuu gumaash jahiz min wen?
        Okot tai sukeer biyuu gumaash jahiz min dukaan geriib.
        Okot taki sukeer biyuu gumaash jahiz min dukaan geriib miteen?
        Okot tai sukeer biyuu gumaash jahiz min dukaan geriib fi yom
        lahad.

    b. Humon ruwa fi beled tomon.
        Munuu ruwa fi beled tomon?
        Akwaana ta Phillip ruwa fi beled tomon.
        Akwaana ta Phillip ruwa fi beled tomon ma munuu?
        Akwaana ta Phillip ruwa fi beled tomon ma jidi tomon.
        Akwaana ta Phillip ruwa fi beled tomon ma jidi tomon miteen?
        Akwaana ta Phillip ruwa fi beled tomon ma jidi tomon gabulu iti-
        niin shahar.

    c. Huwo kulu yom bi alabu kura.
        Munuu kulu yom bi alabu kura?

Welid kalti tai kulu yom alabu kura.
Welid kalti taki kulu yom alabu kura ma munuu?
Welid kalti tai kulu yom alabu kura ma sabii to.
Welid kalti taki kulu yom alabu kura ma sabii to wen?
Welid kalti tai kulu yom alabu kura ma sabii to fi teriig gidaam bet tomon.

d. Humon ashrubu bun ta Januub Sudaan.
Munuu ashrubu bun ta Januub Sudaan?
Kawajaat ashrubu bun ta Januub Sudaan.
Kawajaat ashrubu bun ta Januub Sudaan kam dor?
Kawajaat ashrubu bun ta Januub Sudaan dor wahid bes.
Kawajaat ashrubu bun ta Januub Sudaan dor wahid bes wen?
Kawajaat ashrubu bun to Januub Sudaan dor wahid bes fi bet jeraan tomon.

Kelimaat

agra	'read'
Almaania	'Germany'
form	'form'; cf. worniik
garbiiya	'western'
jinis	'nationality'
mala	'fill in'
munaazama	'organization'
nihaaya	'finally, lastly'
nota	'notebook'
pasport	'passport'
shargiiya	'eastern'
tamantaasher	'eighteen'
waziifa	'occupation'
worniik	'form'; cf. form
yani	'that is to say; i.e.'
ziraa	'agriculture'
zol indu fikra	'expert, specialist'

Asilaat le temriin

1. Munuu deru mala form de?
2. Munuu ma arifu agra Arabi?
3. Zol Januub Sudaani arifu katibu Arabi?
4. Munuu yauu mala form le kawaaja de?
5. Kawaaja amulu fogo damga u be kam?

6. Isim ta kawaaja de munuu?
7. Jinis ta kawaaja de shunuu?
8. Waziifa ta kawaaja de shunuu, yani huwo shagaal shunuu?
9. Nimira pasport ta kawaaja de kam?
10. Anwaan ta kawaaja de shunuu, yani huwo shagaal wen?
11. Kawaaja de ja fi Januub Sudaan ini miteen?
12. Waziifa taki shunuu hasi de fi Januub Sudaan ini?
13. Ita arifu katibu Arabi hasi de?
14. Nas Januub Sudaniin arifu katibu Arabi ketiir?
15. Ita fi Januub Sudaan ini gi ishtaagal ma munaazama shunuu?
16. Ita fi mahaal shokol taki indu fikra fi shokol shunuu?
17. Seii, ita yom tani mala form fi Juba ini?
18. Jinis taki shunuu?
19. Ita indu nota, shokol ta nota shunuu?

Deris nimira tisataasher   Lesson 19
Fi dukaan ta shanta   At the bag shop

Kalaam fi dukaan ta shanta
(Z: zabuun, S: sidu dukaan)

'Dialogue at the bag shop'
(Z: 'customer', S: 'shopkeeper')

Z: Ita bi amulu shanta jilid?
'Do you make leather bags?'

S: Ai, ita deru kam shanta?
'Yes, how many bags do you want?'

Z: Hasab taman to.
'That depends on the price.'

S: Ana bi wodii itiniin del be sebeyiin jinee le anu ita zabuun tai.
'I'll give you those two for seventy pounds because you are a regular customer.'

Z: Del kweis, lakiin ana indu jilid. Ana biyuu min Meriidi. Mumkin ita bi amulu le ana shanta min huwo?
'Those are nice, but I have some leather here. I bought it in Maridi. Can you make me a bag from it?'

S: Ai, mumkin. Ita deru be ida tawiil wala guseer?
'Yes, I can. Do you want it with a long or short handle?'

Z: Guseer. Amulu gumaash fi juwa to tegiil u keitu kweis.
'Short. Make the lining from thick cloth and sew it well.'

S: Kweis. Kayaata to be kamsa jinee u gumaash be ishriin jinee. Kulu sebeyiin jinee.
'Right. The sewing costs five pounds and cloth for the lining is twenty pounds. The total is seventy pounds.'

Z: Nagisu shweya. Ana zabuun taki.
'Reduce it a little. I'm your regular customer.'

S: Kweis, jibu sitiin jinee.
'All right. Give me sixty pounds.'

Z: Ana bi ja shilu miteen?
'When shall I come to collect it?'

S: Taal yom arbaa al jay.
'Come next Wednesday.'

109

Kelimaat ziada al der arufu

1. *Le anu* 'because' is more classical but is sometimes used instead of the more common *ashaan*.

2. Object pronouns are the same as subject pronouns.

Huwo nadii ana.	'He called me.'
Huwo nadii ita.	'He called you *(sg)*.'
Huwo nadii huwo.	'He called him/her/it.'
Huwo nadii aniina.	'He called us.'
Huwo nadii itakum.	'He called you *(pl)*.'
Huwo nadii humon.	'He called them.'

3. The object pronoun *huwo* is usually shortened to *u* and merged with verb-final *u*. However, it is sometimes heard as a longer *u* or as *u* following a verb-final *a*, e.g., *agrau* 'I read it'. Practice positive and negative replies: *Ai, ana ainu; La', ana ma ainu.*

   a. | | |
   |---|---|
   | Ita ainu galam? | Ai, ana ainu. |
   | Ita bi ashrubu shay? | Ai, ana bi ashrubu. |
   | Ita bi amulu shanta jilid? | Ai, ana bi amulu. |
   | Biniiya keitu jalabiiya de? | Ai, huwo keitu. |
   | Katib sejilu zerif al kebiir? | Ai, huwo sejilu. |
   | Ita bi wodii itiniin del? | Ai, ana bi wodii. |
   | Itakum akulu jibna ta Januub Sudaan? | Ai, aniina akulu. |

   b. | | |
   |---|---|
   | Awlaad gi geni katibu jawabaat? | Ai, humon gi geni katibu. |
   | Humon kasulu esmiinti? | Ai, humon kasulu. |
   | Ita agra form taki? | Ai, ana agrau. |
   | Huwo bi ainu arabiiya abuu to? | Ai, huwo bi ainu. |
   | Ita deru biyuu laham de? | Ai, ana deru biyuu. |
   | Aniina sibu muftaa ma itakum? | Ai, itakum sibu. |

   c. | | |
   |---|---|
   | Itakum bi asma radio kulu yom? | Ai, aniina bi asmau. |
   | Kadaam gi geni amulu mokwa hasi de? | Ai, huwo gi geni amulu. |
   | Lisa ita ma ashrubu leben? | Ai, ana lisa ma ashrubu. |
   | Itakum fata bab? | Ai, aniina fatau. |

Kelimaat

gumaash fi juwa	'lining'
ida	'hand, arm, handle'
jibna	'cheese'
jilid	'leather, skin'
le anu	'because'
nadii	'call'
shanta	'bag, case'
sibu	'leave'
taman	'price' *(n)*
tisataasher	'nineteen'
wodii/wadii	'give, take, lend to'

Asilaat le temriin

1. Munuu gi amulu shanta ta jilid?
2. Sidu shanta kelimu huwo bi wodii itiniin shanta del be kam?
3. Zabuun indu jilid ta shunuu?
4. Zabuun biyuu jilid de min wen?
5. Zabuun deru amulu le huwo shunuu?
6. Kayaata to u gumaash kulu be kam?
7. Huwo bi ja shilu miteen?
8. Ita indu shanta ta jilid wenu?
9. Fi dukaan ta jilid fi Juba ini wen?
10. Ita arifu amulu shanta ta jilid?
11. Munuu biyuu shanta jilid fi Juba?

Deris nimira ishriin
Kalaam be telefoon

Lesson 20
A telephone conversation

Kalaam be telefoon

(Sh: Shariif, D: Daniel, S: sikirteer, J: John)

Sh: Ita katibu jawaab ta budaa fi Nimule?

D: La', ana bi katibu hasi de.

Sh: Kweis, katibu hasi de u sikirteer bi tabau le ita.

D: John fi wizaara durubu le ita telefoon gabulu ashara degaayg.

Sh: Huwo kelimu shunuu?

D: Huwo kelimu huwo bi ruwa le Maridi bukra.

Sh: Ana bi udrubu le huwo. (Huwo gi udrubu telefoon le Wizaara Maliiya.)

S: De Wizaara Maliiya. Ita deru munuu?

Sh: Ana deru wunusu ma John.

S: Kweis.
  (Huwo gi wusulu le John.)

J: Ai, ana John.

Sh: Ai, ana Shariif. Ita durubu le ana gabulu shweya. Fi haja?

'Dialogue by telephone'

(Sh: Shariif, D: Daniel, S: 'secretary', J: John)

'Have you written the letter for the goods at Nimule?'

'No, I will write it now.'

'Good, write it now and the secretary will type it for you.'

'John at the ministry called you on the telephone ten minutes ago.'

'What did he say?'

'He said he will go to Maridi tomorrow.'

'I will call him.'
('He calls the Ministry of Finance.')

'This is the Ministry of Finance. Who do you want?'

'I want to talk with John.'

'Okay.'
('She connects with John.')

'Yes, this is John.'

'Yes, this is Shariif. You called me a while ago. Is there something?'

113

J: Ai, ana gi ruwa le Maridi bukra. Ita bagder jibu waragaat to moshruu' ta ziraa gabulu sa hidaasher?

'Yes, I'm going to Maridi tomorrow. Can you bring the papers of the agricultural project before eleven o'clock?'

Sh: Kweis, ana bi jibu le ita hasi de.

'Fine, I will bring it to you now.'

J: Shukran, ma salaam taki.

'Thank you, goodbye.'

Kelimaat ziada al der arufu

1. The verb *durubu/udrubu* has two forms and several meanings. It typically means one of the following: 'to beat, telephone, ring a bell'. It is said that the two forms are interchangeable, but it is interesting to note that in this text *durubu* is always used for past tense and *udrubu* for present or future tense. Generally, the non-past forms reflect school Arabic.

2. To practice telephone conversations seriously, the student must use a telephone to call the teacher or a friend, eventually moving on to business offices. However, it is also helpful to practice while sitting out of sight of each other, e.g., back to back or on opposite sides of a door.

Kelimaat

budaa	'cargo, goods'
durubu/udrubu	'phone, call, ring (a bell), beat, pound' *(v)*
gabulu	'before'
maliiya	'finance'
moshruu'	'project'
tabau	'type' *(v)*
telefoon	'telephone' *(n)*
wizaara	'ministry'
wusulu	'connect'

Asilaat le temriin

1. Jawaab ta budaa wenu?
2. Sikirteer tabau jawaab le ita?
3. Ita bagder tabau jawaab?
4. Munuu durubu telefoon le Sheriif gabulu ashara degaayg?
5. Ita arifu munuu fi Wizaara Maliiya?
6. Ita arifu munuu fi wizaara tani?
7. Mumkin ita durubu telefoon le huwo?

8. Ita wunusu ma jeraan be Arabi?
9. Mumkin bi wusulu telefoon fi maktab taki?
10. John deru waragaat ta moshruu' shunuu?
11. Kan ita durubu telefoon, ita deru wunusu ma munuu?
12. Ita deru wunusu kalaam shunuu ma huwo?
13. Itakum indu moshruu' shunuu ini?
14. Januub Sudaan indu moshruu' ta ziraa, isim to shunuu?
15. Itakum indu budaa fi Kenya?
16. Fi bet taki fi telefoon nimira to kam?
17. Kan ita indu telefoon fi bet takum, ita bagder wunusu ma sabii taki be telefoon?
18. Munuu deru safiru le El Obeid bukra?
19. Telefonaat fi ketiriin fi Juba ini?
20. Nimira telefoon ta maktab takum kam?

Asilaat le muraaja min deris nimira wahid le ishriin

Review questions from lessons 1–20

1. Ita bi biyuu sukar min wen?
2. Itakum derisu Arabi fi Juba wala fi Yei?
3. Yal taki fi fi bet wala humon rowa le medereesa?
4. Seii, ita geiru gumaash taki nahaar de?
5. Humon deriin asha?
6. Ita deru bed gidaada wala salata?
7. Itakum bi asmau radio fi sa kam kulu yom?
8. Ita min beled de zatu wala min bara?
9. Humon geni fi Januub Sudaan ini ketiir kalis?
10. Kam derisiaat itakum afamu min deris nimira wahid le hadi deris nimira ishriin?
11. Mara taki shagaal bara wala gi geni fi bet?
12. Hisa ta aniina gi badau fi sa kam?
13. Munuu gi salau arabiyaat al karabu?
14. Wazin taki kam kilo?
15. Mumkin ita bagder wunusu be Arabi wala la'?
16. Ita indu kam shuhuur fi Januub Sudaan ini?
17. Seii huwo ainu haywanaat ketiir fi Juba?
18. Isim taki munuu?
19. Ita gi ishtaagal ma munaazama UN wala munaazama tani?
20. Mara taki gi ishtaagal fi bet baraau wala fi zol gi saaidu huwo fi bet?
21. Ita indu akwaana?
22. Ita bi arifu agra Arabi?

117

23. Ita gi biyuu laham de min wen?
24. Ita bi rowa fi maktab badi bukra wala ita bi geni fi bet?
25. Lonaat ta bahar shunuu?
26. Awal mara ita rowa fi suk Kongo Kongo de kan miteen?
27. Munuu sejilu gon fi kura gadam? Jenaa ta yamiin wala dib?
28. Munuu udrubu telefoon le Sheriif?
29. Nas lazim bi amulu form ketiir fi ayaam de?
30. Fi haja tehet terebeeza?
31. Kalti Samya bi ishtaagal baraau ketiir wala indu kadaam?
32. Ita deru rowa le Nimule?
33. Okot taki tawiil kalis min rajil to wala huwo guseer?
34. Nas wizaara shilu pasport taki?
35. Munuu lahib jediid fi kura gadam? Jenaa wala dib?
36. Diyuuf min Faraansa akulu gada ma itakum?
37. Shahar shunuu bi kun fi turaab ketiir?
38. Ita geni fi Januub Sudaan ketiir kalis?
39. Lazim ita bi alimu kulu kelimaat fi derisiaat del?

Deris nimira wahid u ishriin   Lesson 21
Fi jineena ta zuhuur   In the flower nursery

Kalaam fi jineena ta zuhuur

(Z: zabuun, S: sidu jineena)

'Dialogue in the flower nursery'

(Z: 'customer', S: 'nurseryman')

Z: Fi le itakum zuhuur ta biyuu?

S: Ai, kulu zuhuur tehet shejara de ta biyuu. Ita deru shunuu?

Z: Ana deru zuhuur sukeer amer. Ita-kum indu zuhuur min shikil to?

S: Fi shejara zuhuur sukeer ini. Kan fi zuhuur to jemiil lakiin zol tani biyuu umbaari.

Z: Ana indi zuhuur lon to abiyad. Amer mafi le ita?

S: Fi, ita ma ainu ben zuhuur asfar u zuhuur bembi?

Z: Ai, ana ainu. Kalaas, ana bi shilu huwo u kamaan shejara zuhuur abiyad.

S: Ita deru tani shunuu?

Z: Ana kan indi shejara zuhuur ketiir ze del, lakiin karabu, tala gowi. De ashaan shunuu?

S: Huwo tala gowi baraau?

Z: Ai, tala gowi baraau.

'Do you have flowers for sale?'

'Yes, all the flowers under this tree are for sale. What do you want?'

'I want small red flowers. Do you have flowers like that?'

'There is a shrub of small flowers here. There were pretty flowers from it but someone bought them yesterday.'

'I have white flowers. Don't you have any red ones?'

'Yes, didn't you see it between the yellow and the pink flowers?'

'Yes, I saw it. Okay, I'll take it and also the shrub with white flowers.'

'Do you want anything else?'

'I had a tree with lots of flowers like that, but it is ruined, it dried up. What caused this?'

'Did it just wither by itself?'

'Yes, it just withered by itself.'

S: Mumkin ita ma kubu le huwo moya ketiir.   'Perhaps you didn't water it enough.'

Z: Shukran le ita, ana gi ruwa.   'Thank you, I am going.'

S: Afwan le ita kamaan.   'You are welcome.'

Kelimaat

abiyad	'white'
amer	'red'
asfar	'yellow'
aswad	'black'
bembi	'pink'
dura	'sorghum'
gowi	'dried up, hard'
kubu	'pour'
shejara	'tree, shrub'
shikil	'shape, kind'
ta biyuu	'for sale'
tala gowi	'wither, dry up'
zarau	'grow, plant'
ze	'like, as'
zuhuur	'flower, plant'

Asilaat le temriin

1. Fi zuhuur fi jineena taki?
2. Ita deru zuhuur shikil shunuu?
3. Ita jibu zuhuur min wen?
4. Fi zuhuur ta biyuu fi Juba?
5. Fi zuhuur fi dar riyaada? Fi shunuu hinaak?
6. Zuhuur sukeer amer isim shunuu be Ingliizi?
7. Zuhuur shunuu jemiil kalis le ita?
8. Gemiis taki lon to shunuu?
9. Gemiis to lon to shunuu?
10. Fi oda de fi shunuu lon to bembi? Abiyad? Asfar?
11. Le shunuu shejara tala gowi?
12. Fi wokit sukun ita kubu moya ketiir wala moya shweya?
13. Fi wokit barid ita ashrubu moya ketiir wala shweya?
14. Ita deru zarau zuhuur wala manga wala dura?
15. Seii Wizaara Maliiya ziraa shunuu?
16. Fi moshruu' zuhuur fi Januub Sudaan ini?
17. Nas munuu lon asfar? Lon amer? Lon abiyad?

Deris nimira itiniin u ishriin   Lesson 22
Fi bet   At home

Kalaam fi bet

(A: Awaatif, N: Nadia, M: Maria, S: Sara)

(Fi motbak)

A: Ita gi geni amulu shunuu?

N: Ana gi geni rakabu mulaah laham. Fi shunuu?

A: Magaas wenu? Ana deru gatau shaar ta Maria.

N: Ana kutu fi martaba taki. Ita ma ainu?

A: La', ana bi ruwa ainu hasi de.
   (Huwo gi ruwa)

N: (le Maria) Jibu le ana sikiin u malaga. Ana deru jeribu ruz de.

M: Yauu de. Muna lisa gi geni nedifu osh? Gabulu nus sa huwo kelimu huwo gi ruwa le hamaam.

N: Huwo kaslaan. Huwo sibu mugshaasha u huwo gi geni agrau jeriida.

'Dialogue in the house'

(A: Awaatif, N: Nadia, M: Mary, S: Sarah)

('In the kitchen')

'What are you doing?'

'I am cooking stewed meat. What's the matter?'

'Where are the scissors? I want to cut Mary's hair.'

'I put them on your bed. Didn't you see them?'

'No, I'll go look now.'

('She goes out.')

'(to Mary) Bring me a knife and spoon. I want to taste this rice.'

'Here. Is Muna still cleaning the yard? More than half an hour ago she said she was going to take a bath.'

'She is lazy. She left the broom and is sitting reading a magazine.'

M: O, maleesh, ana zekiru fi zol wodii   'Oh, sorry, I remember there was
le ana kitaab u kelimu nowodii le   a person who gave me a book and
huwo. Lakiin lisa ana ma wodii le   told me to give it to her. But I still
huwo.   have not given it to her.'
(Huwo gi ruwa)   ('She goes out.')

S: (Gi dakulu) Maleesh, kahraba gata.   '(Entering) Sorry, the electricity is
Ana ma bagder mokwa fustaan tai.   cut off. I can't iron my dress.'

N: Kahraba gata? Fatau talaaja. De   'Is the electricity cut off? Open
wokit ana bi nedifu talaaja de.   the refrigerator. This is the time
                                             for me to clean it.'

S: Kweis, mumkin ana bagder saaidu   'Okay, may I help you?'
ita?

N: Kweis, ma bataal, taal saaidu ana.   'Okay, not bad, come help me.'

Kelimaat ziada al der arufu

In an indirect quotation, the subject 'I' or 'we' is expressed by the prefix *ni*
instead of the pronoun *ana* or *aniina*. In the dialogue, *ni-wodii* 'me to give'
is spelled *nowodii* to show assimilation of /i/ to the following /o/. (Listen
for other cases of assimilation as well.)

John kelimu (le ana/aniina) ...   'John told me/us...'
    niakulu akil de.   'to eat this food.'
    niamulu akil ta gada.
    nishiilu kitaab de le huwo.
    noruwa le suk nibiyuu laham.
    nidurubu haywaan dak.
    niresimu sura jemiil.

Kelimaat

faham	'charcoal'
hamaam	'bathroom'
jaz	'gas'
jaz abiyad	'kerosene, paraffin'
jeribu	'taste'
jeriida	'magazine'
kahraba	'electricity'
kaslaan	'lazy'
kitaab (*pl* kitabaat)	'book'
kutu	'put'

leyin	'soft'
magaas	'scissors'
malaga	'spoon'
martaba	'bed, mattress'
mugshaasha	'broom'
mulaa(h)	'stew, sauce'
no-/ni-	'told me to'
rakabu	'cook'
shaar/shahar	'hair'
sikiin	'knife'
siniin	'sharp'
talaaja	'refrigerator'
telij	'ice'

Asilaat le temriin

1. Ita gi geni amulu shunuu?
2. Ita rakabu shunuu?
3. Ita deru akulu mulaah laham wala mulaah kudruwaat?
4. Ita arifu gatau shaar?
5. Ita gatau shaar be shunuu?
6. Nas amulu martaba ashaan shunuu?
7. Martaba taki gowi wala leyin?
8. Pam kutu galam to wen?
9. Fi bet taki fi sikiin siniin?
10. Ita amulu shunuu be malaga?
11. Ita deru akulu ruz baraau wala be mulaah?
12. Kan ita rakabu mulaah ita jeribu ma ida wala ma malaga?
13. Lazim bi nedifu osh ketiir wala bi nedifu hamaam ketiir?
14. Osh taki fi shunuu fogo?
15. Gabulu sa wahid ita bi amulu shunuu?
16. Munuu kaslaan?
17. Ita sibu mugshaasha wen?
18. Ita agrau jeriida kulu yom fi sa kam?
19. Ita agrau kam kitaabaat fi kulu usbuu?
20. Yauu de kitaab, wodii le Maria.
21. Ana kelimu le ita amulu shunuu? (Ita kelimu nowodii le huwo.)
22. Fi bet taki fi kahraba kulu yom?
23. Kulu yom kahraba bi gata sa kam?
24. Ita rakabu akil be kahraba wala be jaz?
25. Fi bet taki fi mokwa ta kahraba wala ta faham?
26. Talaaja bi kun barid be kahraba wala be jaz abiyad, u kef?
27. Kan kahraba gata, ita bi nedifu talaaja?

28. Nas kutu shunuu fi talaaja? U amulu shunuu fi talaaja?
29. Nas bi amulu shunuu ma mugshaasha?
30. Ita deru rakabu akil wala nedifu hamaam wala mokwa fustaan?

Deris nimira talaata u ishriin Lesson 23
Ojora bet   Renting a house

Kalaam ta ojora bet
(Z: zol ta ojora, S: sid bet)

'Dialogue about renting a house'
(Z: 'renter', S: 'landlord')

Z: Fi zol kelimu le ana ita indu bet ta ojora.

'A person told me you have a house for rent.'

S: Sah. Ita deru ajoru bet de?

'True. Do you want to rent it?'

Z: Ai, bet bitaniina sukeer.

'Yes, our house is too small.'

S: Ita deru kam oda?

'How many rooms do you want?'

Z: Ana deru talaata odaat u oda juluus.

'I want three rooms and a parlor.'

S: Ana indu talaata odaat u juwa ta arabiiya u jineena kweis.

'I have three rooms, a carport and a nice garden.'

Z: Fi yatuu hay?

'In which district?'

S: Fi hay Malakaal.

'In Malakal district.'

Z: Bet de fi fogo seriir u terebeeza u kursiyaat u dolaab, wala mafi?

'Does this house have beds, a table and a cupboard, or not?'

S: Fi Juba biyuut ta ojora mafi hajaat de, lakiin bet de fi kahraba u fi mustraa u fi masuura. Ana indu bet tani gi abunoo fi hay Buluk. Bi kun fogo oda hamaam.

'In Juba rent houses don't have these things, but this house has electricity, a toilet and a faucet. I have another house being built in Buluk District. It will have a bathroom in it.'

Z: Bet dak bi kun jahiz miteen?

'When will that house be ready?'

S: Mumkin bi kun jahiz fi shahar tisa.

'It may be ready in September.'

Z: Bet de gediim fi fogo maruwaa wala mukaayif hawa?

'Does this old house have fans or air coolers?'

125

S: Fi fogo itiniin mukaayif hawa. Ita kan deru ana bi worii le ita bet de hasi de?   'It has two air coolers. Do you want me to show it to you now?'

Z: Kweis, aniina ruwa hasi de.   'Okay, let's go now.'

S: Yanuu de bet. Fadal, aniina dakulu.   'Here is the house. Go ahead, let's go in.'

Z: Bet de kweis kalis. Ojora to be kam fi shahar?   'This house is very good. How much is its rent per month?'

S: Itiniin alf jinee fi shahar.   'Two thousand pounds per month.'

Z: Ketiir kalis. Nagisu shweya.   'Too much. Lower it a little.'

S: Kalaas, ita bi dafau alf khamsa miya jinee fi shahar.   'Okay, you will pay one thousand, five hundred pounds per month.'

Z: Kweis, ma bataal, shukran le ita.   'Okay, not bad, thank you.'

Kelimaat

abunoo	'build/built'
ajoru	'rent' *(v)*
bi kun	'will be, because'
bileel	'night'
Buluk	'Buluk District in Juba'
haraami	'thief'
hawa	'air'
hay	'district'
juwa ta arabiiya	'carport (lit. inside place for cars)'
maruwaa/muruwaa	'fan (for cooling air)'
masuura	'water tap'
mukaayif hawa	'evaporation cooler'
mustraa/musturaa	'toilet'
ojora	'rent' *(n)*
seriir	'bed frame'
ta ojora	'for rent'
worii	'show'
yatuu	'which'

Asilaat le temriin

1. Nas fi beled bi ajoru bet?
2. Nas fi Juba indu bet wala ajoru bet ketiir?
3. Fi Juba ajoru bet be kam jinee kulu shahar?
4. Munuu indu bet ta ojora?
5. Ita deru ajoru bet sukeer wala kebiir? Kam odaat?
6. Ita deru yatuu oda?

7. Bet taki fi yatuu hay?
8. Fi Juba bet ta ojora fi fogo seriir u terebeeza?
9. Bet ta ojora fi fogo shunuu?
10. Ita jibu dolaab min wen? Fi dukaan ta dolaab?
11. Ita deru ajoru bet gi abunoo? Le?
12. Kulu bet fi Juba fi masuura fogo?
13. Kef nas bi jibu moya?
14. Kulu bet fi kahraba fogo? Kef nas bi ainu bileel?
15. Bet gi abunoo bi kun jahiz miteen?
16. Fustaan gi keitu bi kun jahiz miteen? Kam yom?
17. Bet taki fi fogo shunuu ashaan amulu barid?
18. Ita deru maruwaa wala mukaayif hawa? Le?
19. Kan ita deru ajoru bet, ita deru sidu bet worii le ita awal shunuu?
20. Kan rajil bi ajoru bet, mara to lazim bi ainu awal?
21. Ita bi ainu bet ta ojora, ita bi ainu shunuu?
22. Bet gediim indu mustraa?
23. Bet jediid indu mukaayif hawa?
24. Ita deru worii bet taki le haraami?
25. Munuu gi ajoru bet taki, ita ajoru wala munaazama ajoru le ita?
26. Fi beled taki ojora ta bet itiniin alf jinee fi shahar wala kam?
27. Fi beled taki bet ta ojora fi fogo kahraba u masuura?
28. Fi Juba nas ajoru bet sukeer be kam jinee fi shahar?
29. Bet sukeer indu kam odaat?
30. Nas abunoo bet sukeer be kam jinee?
31. Ita deru num fog martaba, wala seriir, wala kulu?
32. Ita bagder num fi kursi? Fi hisa Arabi?
33. Bet taki fi fogo masuura?
34. Munuu arifu abunoo bet?
35. Hawa fi bet taki kef: sukun wala barid?
36. Worii le ana kitaab taki, galam taki, kursi taki.

Deris nimira arba u ishriin — Lesson 24
Zowiju — A wedding

Kalaam ta zowiju

(N: Nura, M: Maria)

N: Ya Maria, ita ainu zowiju fi Januub Sudaan ini?

M: La', zowiju kef fi Januub Sudaan ini?

N: Kweis kalis. Awal yom rajil bi dafau guruush le ahal ta biniiya.

Wa yom nimira itiniin yom hafla zowiju.
Biniiya bi libisu gumaash abiyad u rajil bi libisu kot.
Humon bi ruwa fi kaniisa le salawaat.
Min hinaak humon bi ruwa le istiidiu ashaan sowru.
Wa min istiidiu humon bi lifu juwa Juba be arabiyaat.
Wa min hinaak humon bi ruwa le mahaal hafla.

M: Fi kaniisa humon bi amulu shunuu?

'Dialogue about a wedding'

(N: Nura, M: Maria)

'Maria, have you seen a wedding in South Sudan?'

'No, how is a wedding here in South Sudan?'

'Very nice. On the first day the man will pay money to the family of the girl.
On the second day is the wedding party day.
The girl will wear white cloth and the man will wear a coat.
They will go to the church to pray.

From there they will go to the studio for pictures.
From the studio they will wind through Juba in cars.
Then they will go to the place of the party.'

'What do they do in the church?'

129

N: Awal humon bi seli le Rabuuna, wa badi dak abuuna bi kelimu le humon kelii humon geni kweis biduun mashaakil.

'First they will pray to God, and after that the pastor will tell them to behave themselves well without problems.'

M: Sabii ta mara u ta rajil bi amulu kef?

'What will the friends of the woman and the man do?'

N: Sabii ta mara u ta rajil bi wodii guruush le humon. Wa taniin bi wodii zuhuur le humon.

'The friends of the woman and the man will give money to them. And others give flowers to them.'

M: Fi mahaal hafla nas munuu bi bada alabu?

'At the party place which people will begin dancing?'

N: Rajil al zowiju biniiya humon bi alabu awal, badeen bagi nas bi ja alabu wara.

'The groom will dance first, then the rest of the people dance behind.'

M: Hafla de bi alabu le hadi sa kam?

'At this party until what time will they dance?'

N: Rajil al zowiju biniiya humon bi ruwa fi sa itnaasher bileel u bagi nas bi alabu le hadi sabaa.

'The groom and bride will go at midnight and the rest of the people will dance until morning.'

M: Shukran le kalaam taki, ya Nura.

'Thank you for your talk, Nura.'

N: Afwan le ita, ya Maria.

'You're welcome, Maria.'

Kelimaat ziada al der arufu

1. A wedding is also called *iris,* though the verb *zowiju* is used more.

2. Notice the construction *Rajil al zowiju biniiya, humon...* 'The man who marries the girl, they...'

Kelimaat

abuuna	'pastor, priest'
afashaat	'baggage, luggage'
alabu	'dance, play'
bagi	'remainder'
biduun	'without'
iris	'wedding'
istiidiu	'studio'
kaniisa/keniisa	'church'
kelii	'cause'
kot	'coat'
libisu	'put on, wear'
lifu	'circle around'

mashaakil (*pl* mushkila)	'trouble, problem'
salaa (*pl* salawaat)	'prayer'
seli	'pray'

Asilaat le temriin

1. Munuu ainu zowiju fi Januub Sudaan ini?
2. Zowiju fi Januub Sudaan ini kef?
3. Rajil Januub Sudaani bagder zowiju itiniin wala telaata biniyaat, wala wahid wahid bes?
4. Rajil Ameriiki bagder zowiju itiniin wala telaata biniyaat?
5. Fi Januub Sudaan ini kan rajil zowiju biniiya, lazim bi dafau guruush?
6. Rajil al zowiju lazim bi dafau guruush le nas munuu?
7. Yom nimira itiniin yom shunuu fi iris?
8. Biniiya bi libisu shunuu? Rajil bi libisu shunuu?
9. Rajil u biniiya ruwa wen? U tani wen?
10. Fi kaniisa humon amulu shunuu?
11. Abuuna bi kelimu shunuu le humon?
12. Munuu amulu sura, u wen?
13. Sabii ta mara u ta rajil bi amulu kef?
14. Kam yom rajil u mara bi geni biduun mashaakil?
15. Munuu gi geni biduun mashaakil?
16. Le shunuu fi mashaakil?
17. Le shunuu lazim nas bi seli le Rabuuna?
18. Fi mahaal hafla nas munuu bi bada alabu?
19. Munuu ainu alabu ta Januub Sudaan ini? Nas Januub Sudaniin gi alabu kef?
20. Rajil al zowiju biniiya humon bi alabu le hadi sa kam?
21. Badeen humon ruwa wen?
22. Ita deru alabu le hadi sa itnaasher wala le hadi sabaa?
23. Nas bi ruwa le kaniisa kulu usbuu fi yom yatuu?
24. Nas bi amulu shunuu fi kaniisa?
25. Abuuna bi amulu shunuu fi kaniisa?
26. Kan ita ma indu guruush, ita bagder zowiju biniiya?
27. Bad ma dafau guruush le abuu ta biniiya, ita bi amulu shunuu ma bagi guruush?
28. Kan ita zowiju biniiya ita bi kun indu bagi guruush?
29. Kan ita indu itiniin alf jinee u badeen ita dafau ojora ta bet alf u orbomiiya jinee, bagi kam jinee?
30. Kan ita alabu le hadi sabaa, ita bagder ruwa le shokol?
31. Rajil u biniiya bi lifu fi Juba be shunuu? Le?
32. Fi beled nas bi lifu be shunuu? Be gadam?
33. Ita ruwa le istiidiu amulu shunuu?

34. Biniiya bagder zowijuu ligoo indu kam sena? U rajil?
35. Mumkin, ita bi safiru biduun guruush?
36. Mumkin, ita bi safiru biduun afashaat?

Deris nimira kamsa u ishriin   Lesson 25
Mutu (1)   Death (1)

Kalaam ta mutu	'Dialogue about death'
(J: John, M: Moses)	(J: John, M: Moses)

J: Ita ja min wen, ya Moses?
'Where have you come from, Moses?'

M: Ana ja min bet ta akuu abuu tai fi mahaal bika.
'I have come from the house of my father's brother at the place of mourning.'

J: Kafaara le ita. Munuu yauu mutu?
'Sympathy to you. Who died?'

M: Kafaara Alaa, jidi tai yauu mutu.
'God's sympathy, my grandfather died.'

J: Huwo kan ayaan be waja dahar wala ayaan be shunuu?
'Had he been sick from backache or what was he sick from?'

M: Huwo ayaan be ayaan to min bedri. De waja dahar.
'He was sick from long ago. It was back pain.'

J: Itakum kan wodii huwo le diktoor?
'Had you taken him to the doctor?'

M: Aniina wodii huwo le diktoor u diktoor keshifu huwo.
'We took him to the doctor and the doctor examined him.'

J: Huwo mutu miteen?
'When did he die?'

M: Huwo mutu nahaar de geriib sabaa. Ana gi ruwa fi bet kal tai.
'He died today at almost morning. I am going to the house of my mothers's brother.'

J: Kweis, ana bi ja ruwa badeen fi mahaal bika de.
'Okay, I will be going after a while to this place of mourning.'

M: Kweis, ma salaam taki.
'Okay, goodbye.'

J: Ma salaam taki kamaan.
'Goodbye to you too.'

Kelimaat ziada al der arufu

1. Though *Abuu tai* is more common, some use *abuuy* for 'my father'.

2. *Mahaal bika* or *mahaal mutu* can be used of the house where there is mourning; however, *bika* is not used as a verb in Juba Arabic. *Kori/kore* is used for 'cry, mourn'.

3. *Kafaara* is the appropriate term of sympathy when there is death or serious illness, not *maleesh*.

4. Notice the use of *bi ja ruwa* together, 'I will be going'.

Kelimaat

abuuy	'my father'
Alaa(h)	'God'
bika	'mourning'
diktoor	'doctor'
keshifu	'examine'
kori/kore	'cry, mourn'
mutu	'die, death'

Asilaat le temriin

1. Ya sabii, Moses ja min wen?
2. Mahaal bika mana to shunuu?
3. Mahaal bika wenu?
4. Kan zol mutu, ita kelimu shunuu? Maleesh?
5. Jidi taki kef?
6. Abuuba taki kef?
7. Kulu zol ayaan bi mutu?
8. Ita kan ayaan be waja dahar?
9. Dahar taki kef hasi de?
10. Akuu taki isim to munuu?
11. Abuu taki isim to munuu?
12. Akuu abuu taki isim to munuu?
13. Kan jidi taki ayaan, ita wodii huwo le diktoor?
14. Diktoor bi amulu shunuu? Le shunuu?
15. Kulu nas bi ruwa le diktoor, bi kun kweis?
16. Bad ma diktoor keshifu zol, huwo lazim amulu shunuu?
17. Munuu dafau guruush?
18. Zol mutu bagder dafau guruush?

19. Munuu kal taki? Isim to munuu?
20. Ita bi kafu min zol al mutu? Le?
21. Le shunuu nas mutu?
22. Ita bi kafu min ayaan?
23. Nas bi mutu be arabiiya kef?
24. Ita bi kafu min arabiiya?
25. Le shunuu nas bi kafu min mutu?
26. Bad ma nas kan mutu, humon indu waja tani?
27. Le shunuu nas ruwa le mahaal bika?
28. Humon ruwa le mahaal bika kam yom?
29. Zol bagder mutu bad kam sena?
30. Zol mutu indu mashaakil? Ahal to indu mashaakil? Kef?
31. Kan zol mutu, ahal to bika wala kori?

Deris nimira sita u ishriin   Lesson 26
Mutu (2)   Death (2)

Kalaam ta mutu
(M: Moses, J: John)

M: Ya John, umbaari ita ruwa wen?

J: Umbaari ana ruwa fi mahaal bika.

M: Kafaara le ita. Munuu yauu mutu?

J: Kafaara Alaa. Jena ta kal tai yauu mutu.

M: Huwo mutu be ayaan shunuu?

J: Huwo kan ayaan gisim to gi mofogu.

M: Itakum kan wadii le diktoor?

J: Ai, aniina wadii huwo le diktoor u diktoor keshifu huwo.

M: Diktoor ligoo le huwo ayaan shunuu?

J: Ligoo le huwo gisim mofogu u tani dom to shweya.

M: Seii, wadii le huwo dawaat?

J: Diktoor wadii le huwo dawaat lakiin ma amulu le huwo haja.

M: Badeen itakum amulu kef?

J: Aniina rija huwo fi bet.

'Dialogue about death'
(M: Moses, J: John)

'John, where did you go yesterday?'

'Yesterday I went to the place of mourning.'

'Sympathies to you. Who died?'

'Sympathies of God. The daughter of my mother's brother died.'

'What sickness did she die from?'

'She was sick from a rash.'

'Did you take her to the doctor?'

'Yes, we took her to the doctor and the doctor examined her.'

'What sickness did the doctor find?'

'It was found that her body broke out in a rash and she also had little blood.'

'Truly, was she given medicine?'

'The doctor gave medicines to her but they didn't do anything.'

'Then what did you do?'

'We returned her home.

137

Badeen abuu to biyuu ganamooya u nadii ahal ashaan ja ainu kalaam ta ayaan.

Then her father bought a goat and called the family in order to examine the cause of the sickness.

Badeen dabaau ganamooya u nihaaya ahal ligoo abuu u uma ta jena humon gi kori-kori.

Then he sacrificed the goat and finally the family found that the father and mother of the child argued.

Nas ahal kelimu kelii humon geni kweis ashaan humon indu jena sukeer.

People of the families told them to behave themselves because they had a small child.'

M: Badeen hasil shunuu?

'Then what happened?'

J: Humon asma kalaam de u jena biga kweis.

'They listened to these words and the child became well.

Badeen humon rija kori-kori tani.

Then they returned to arguing again.

Mara to rija fi bet ta ahal tomon ma jena to kulu.

His wife returned to her family's house with her child for good.

Min hinaak ayaan ja tani amsiku jena to yala jena to ja mutu.

From there the sickness came again and held her child until she died.'

M: Badeen nas ta ahal amulu kef?

'Then what did the families do?'

J: Yom nimira wahid nas kori u shilu jena ruwa dofunu.

'On the first day people mourned and took the child and buried her.

Yom nimira itiniin ahal ta mara ja u ahal ta rajil kamaan wa humon wunusu gediiya, lakiin ma kalasu.

On the second day the wife's family came and the man's family too and they held trial, discussing it, but it wasn't resolved.

Yom nimira telaata humon dabaau kuruuf u akulu u wunusu gediiya ja ligoo abuu ta jena galtaan.

On the third day they sacrificed a sheep, ate it, and discussed until they found that the girl's father was guilty.

Kelii huwo biyuu kuruuf u kelii dabaau ashaan kelii humon geni kweisiin.

They let him buy a sheep and kill it in order to allow them to live well.'

M: Kalaam de kalasu?

'Now is it resolved?'

J: Ai, kalaam de kalasu. Kal tai biga kweis ma mara to.

'Yes, it's resolved. My uncle has become good with his wife.'

Kelimaat ziada al der arufu

1. *Ahal* 'family' and *beled* 'country' must be possessed by plurals: *ahal tomon* 'their family', *beled takum* 'your (pl) country'. It is not appropriate to ask someone about "his" or "her" country as if it belonged to him or her alone.

2. *Huwa* is sometimes used instead of *huwo* 'he/she/it' because of influence from Classical Arabic.

3. The verb *ja* 'come' sometimes has an aspectual meaning 'until' when used together with another verb, as in the following examples:

jena to ja mutu	'until her daughter died'
wunusu gediiya ja ligoo abuu ta	'held court until they found that
jena galtaan.	the child's father was guilty.'

Kelimaat

amsiku	'hold, take'
asma	'listen, obey, hear'
dabaau	'slaughter, sacrifice' *(v)*
dawa (*pl* dawaat)	'medicine'
dofunu	'bury'
dom	'blood'
galtaan	'guilty'
ganamooya	'goat'
gediiya	'court trial'
hasil	'happen'
kalaam	'matter, case'
kori-kori	'argue'
kuruuf (*pl* kurufaat)	'sheep'
ligoo	'find, discover'
mofogu	'break out in rash'
yala	'until'

Asilaat le temriin

1. Munuu yauu umbaari ruwa fi mahaal bika?
2. Jena ta kal ta munuu yauu mutu?
3. Huwo mutu be ayaan shunuu?
4. Humon kan wadii jena de le diktoor wala la'?
5. Kan jena taki ayaan ita bi wadii huwa le diktoor?
6. Diktoor ligoo le jena de ayaan shunuu?
7. Seii, diktoor wadii le jena de dawaat?
8. Badeen humon amulu kef le jena de?
9. Seii, ahal ta mara u ta rajil ja ainu kalaam ta jena de?
10. Nas ahal ja ligoo le humon shunuu?
11. Nas ahal ta mara u ta rajil kelimu le humon shunuu fi nihaaya?
12. Seii, humon asma kalaam ta ahal tomon?

13. Badeen humon rija kori-kori wala mafi?
14. Munuu yauu rija fi bet tomon ma jena to?
15. Kalaam shunuu kelii mara de rija fi bet tomon?
16. Badeen fi shunuu hasil le jena de?
17. Seii, humon rija jena de le diktoor tani nimira itiniin?
18. Badeen nas ta ahal amulu kef? Wala shunuu?
19. Yom nimira itiniin fi mahaal bika humon amulu shunuu?
20. Yom nimira telaata fi mahaal bika humon amulu shunuu?
21. Ligoo munuu yauu galtaan?
22. Kelimu le abuu ta jena shunuu fi nihaaya ta bika?
23. Nas gi rowa le diktoor le shunuu?
24. Kan ita ayaan, ita bi rowa le munuu?
25. Seii, ita kan ayaan yom wahid be ayaan shunuu bataal kalis?
26. Munuu kan ayaan awal umbaari fi bet takum?
27. Ayaan shunuu yauu ketiir kalis fi Juba ini?
28. Ayaan shunuu ketiir kalis fi beled taki?
29. Kan itakum kulu ayaaniin fi bet takum wala la'?
30. Ita kan ayaan fi yom lahad al fat?

Deris nimira saba u ishriin   Lesson 27
Safar be tiyaara   Travel by plane

Kalaam ta safir be tiyaara

(Z: zol al deru safir be tiyaara,
K: katib)

Z: Ana deru amulu hejiz le Nairobi fi
   usbuual jay.

K: Ita deru amulu hejiz le kam nas?

Z: Zol wahid bes.

K: Fi le ita taskara?

Z: Ai fi.

K: Tiyaara ta yom itniini mahaal
   mafi. Yom kamiis kweis ma ita?

Z: Kweis. Wazin ta afashaat fi taskara
   le hadi kam kilo?

K: Ishriin kilo bes.

Z: Tiyaara bi gum fi sa kam fi yom
   kamiis?

K: Tiyaara bi gum fi sa tamaanya ila
   tilit fi sabaa.

Z: Wa ana bi ruwa fi mataar fi sa kam?

K: Lazim ita bi ja fi mataar gabulu sa
   sita u nus fi sabaa.

'Dialogue about travel by airplane'

(Z: 'person who wants to travel by
air', K: 'clerk')

'I want to make a reservation to
Nairobi for next week.'

'You want to make a reservation
for how many people?'

'Only one person.'

'Do you have a ticket?'

'Yes, I do.'

'Monday's plane doesn't have
room. Is Thursday okay with you?'

'Okay. Up to how much baggage
weight is included in a ticket?'

'Only twenty kilos.'

'At what time on Thursday does
the plane take off?'

'The plane will take off at 7:40 in
the morning.'

'And what time shall I go to the
airport?'

'You must come to the airport before 6:30 in the morning.'

141

Z: Ana indu sabii tai bi ja min Kahira   'I have my friend coming from
   aleela. Tiyaara ta sa ashara u rubu   Cairo today. Has the 10:15 plane
   ja?   arrived?'
K: Lisa. Huwo bi akir be arba sa-aat.   'Not yet. It will be four hours late.'
Z: Shukran. Ma salaam.   'Thank you. Goodbye.'

Kelimaat

akir	'be late'
ashiiya	'late afternoon, evening'
gum	'take off, get up, wake up, arise'
hejiz	'reservation'
Kahira	'Cairo'
mataar(a)	'airport'
muta-akir	'late' *(adj)*
taskar(a)	'ticket'

Asilaat le temriin

1. Munuu deru amulu hejiz le Nairobi fi usbuu al jay?
2. Fi le ita taskara ta tiyaara hasi de?
3. Kan ita indu taskara ta tiyaara ita bi safiru le wen?
4. Seii, fi yom ita safiru be murkab fi juwa Januub Sudaan ini?
5. Kan ita deru safiru be bas ita bi kun indu taskara?
6. Seii, yom wahid ita safiru le Nairobi be arabiiya wala be tiyaara?
7. Zol kan deru safiru bi amulu hejiz yom kam?
8. Kam dor tiyaara ta Januub Sudaan bi rowa le Nairobi kulu usbuu?
9. Munaazama takum indu tiyaara wala mafi?
10. Munaazama shunuu indu tiyaara fi Juba ini?
11. Kan ita deru safiru le Nairobi ita bi safiru be tiyaara ta munaazama takum?
12. Wazin ta afashaat fi taskar ta tiyaara le hadi kam kilo?
13. Tiyaara ta yom itniini bi ja min Kartuum fi sa kam le Juba ini?
14. Tiyaara ta Januub Sudaan bi rija sa kam min Nairobi le Juba fi yom itniini?
15. Kam sa-aat tiyaara bi amulu min Nairobi le Juba?
16. Kam sa-aat tiyaara bi amulu min Juba le Kahira?
17. Kan tiyaara bi rowa fi sa ashara ita bi rowa le mataar fi sa kam?
18. Kan tiyaara bi rowa le Nairobi bukra ita bi jibu afashaat taki le maktab tiyaara fi sa kam?
19. Seii, ita indu sabii taki bi rowa le Nairobi?
20. Seii, ita indu sabii taki bi ja min Nairobi le Juba?

21. Ita kan deru safiru le Nairobi ita bi rowa le mataara be arabiiya wala bi shilu ita ma arabiiya le mataara?
22. Itakum indu nas bi safiru le Nairobi fi usbuu al jay?
23. Ita indu ahal taki bi ja min beled taki le Juba?
24. Seii, ita ja min beled taki be tiyaara wala be arabiiya le Januub Sudaan ini?
25. Abuu taki fi indu tiyaara sukeer wala mafi?
26. Fi beled takum fi nas bi sala tiyaarat?
27. Seii, fi nas fi beled takum bi sala arabiiyaat?
28. Tiyaara Boeing gi sala wen?
29. Tiyaara ta Januub Sudaan bi ja kulu yom min Kahira le Juba?
30. Seii, fi tiyaara ta beled takum ja fi Januub Sudaan ini? Miteen u wen?

Deris nimira tamaanya u ishriin Lesson 28
Ma diktoor   With the doctor

Kalaam ma diktoor

(D: diktoor, M: mara ajuus,
U: uma weled)

D: Fadal, geni, ya mara ajuus. Fi
   shunuu bataal?

M: Ana ma kweis, ya diktoor. Ana
   indu huma, u ena tai gi waja u dahar tai kamaan gi waja, u gisim tai
   kulu gi waja.

D: Min miteen ita kan ayaan?

M: Min bedri u ana ma arifu ayaan de
   indu kam yom.

D: Fi le ita waja ras?

M: Ai, ana indu waja ras shediid.

D: Shilu dawa de u ashrubu min huwo
   telaata maraat fi yom, u badi akil
   lazim ita bi num.

M: Ana ma bagder akulu akil ta kulu
   kulu, ya diktoor. Haja de gi waja
   shediid.

D: Maleesh. Ashrubu moya ketiir u
   akulu bordokaal.
   (Mara ajuus gi ruwa u mara tani gi
   ja ma weled to.)

'Dialogue with a doctor'

(D: 'doctor', M: 'old lady',
U: 'mother of child')

'Come in and sit down, lady. What
is the trouble?'

'I'm not well, doctor. I have a cold,
my eyes ache and my back also
aches, and my whole body aches.'

'Since when have you been sick?'

'For a long time and I don't know how
many days I've had this sickness.'

'Do you have a headache?'

'Yes, I have a terrible headache.'

'Take this medicine and drink
some of it three times a day, and
after eating you must sleep.'

'I cannot eat food at all, doctor.
This thing aches terribly.'

'I'm sorry. Drink a lot of water and
eat oranges.'

('The old lady goes out and another woman enters with her boy.')

145

U: Weled tai waga min shejara u kureen to awagu.
(Diktoor gi keshifu kureen ta
weled).

'My son fell from a tree and his leg
is injured.'
('The doctor examines the boy's
leg.')

D: Ma kasuru, lakiin fi woroma. Ana
bi lifu ma rabaat. Mata kelii huwo
dowru.

'It isn't broken, but there is swelling. I will wrap it with bandage.
Don't let him walk.'

U: Huwo ma bagder dowru hasi de
ashaan gi waja shediid.

'He cannot walk now because it
hurts terribly.'

D: Kweis. Jibu huwo le ana tani badi
telaata yom.

'Good. Bring him to me again after three days.'

U: Shukran, ya diktoor.

'Thank you, doctor.'

Kelimaat ziada al der arufu

Vowels followed by *de* 'this' often assimilate to the *e*, e.g., *hase de* 'now' and
haje de 'this thing' instead of *hasi de* and *haja de*.

Kelimaat

ajuus	'old'
akiim	'doctor' (older word)
awagu	'injure'
bedri	'long time ago'
disinteerio	'dysentery'
ena	'eyes'
huma	'a cold'
kureen	'leg, foot'
lifu	'wrap'
malaaria	'malaria'
mara (*pl* maraat)	'time'
ras	'head'
robaat/rabaat	'wrapping, bandage'
robutu	'wrap' *(v)*
waga	'fall, fell'
woroma	'swelling'
woromu	'swell' *(v)*

Asilaat le temriin

1. Fi shunuu bataal fi gisim taki?
2. Ita indu huma?
3. Nas indu huma ketiir fi wokit barid wala fi wokit sukun?

4. Ena taki kef?
5. Dahar taki kef?
6. Ita kan ayaan miteen? Ita ayaan hasi de?
7. Ita kan ayaan be malaaria kam yom?
8. Kan ita ayaan be malaaria, ita bi ashrubu dawa shunuu? Be huma? Be waja ras? Be disinteerio?
9. Kan ita ayaan, ita bi akulu bordokaal u bi num badi akil?
10. Mara ajuus fi deris de bagder gi akulu akil zaman huwo ayaan?
11. Munuu yauu waga min shejara?
12. Kureen to kasuru? Kureen to kef?
13. Kan kureen taki kasuru, diktoor lazim bi amulu shunuu?
14. Kan kureen taki awagu u fi woroma, diktoor bi amulu shunuu?
15. Kan weled kasuru wala awagu kureen, mata kelii huwo amulu shunuu?
16. Kan kureen taki waja shediid, ita deru amulu shunuu? Alabu kura?
17. Badi talaata yom mara u weled to bi amulu shunuu?
18. Kan ita indu huma, ita bi lifu rasu taki be robaat?
19. Ita bagder alabu kura ma kureen kasuru?
20. Seii, ayaan ta malaaria fi ketiir fi beled takum wala mafi ta kulu kulu?
21. Fi shejaraat ketiir fi osh takum?
22. Shejara fogo manga isim to shunuu be Arabi?
23. Shejaraat al ketiir kalis fi Juba isim to shunuu?
24. Fi osh takum, itakum indu shejaraat zuhuur?
25. Seii, mangaat ketiir ini wala ketiir fi Yei?
26. Shahar kam fi bordokaal ketiir fi Juba?
27. Ayaan shunuu yauu ketiir fi Juba ini?
28. Seii, awlaad bi waga min shejaraat ketiir wala bi waga zaman humon gi alabu?
29. Seii, yom ita awagu fi kura ta kureen wala la'?
30. Seii, kureen taki kasuru? Wen? U miteen?
31. Fi zol fi bet takum kan ayaan wala kan kureen to kasuru?

Deris nimira tisa u ishriin   Lesson 29
Fi gaba   In the countryside

Kalaam fi gaba

(N: nas al gi safiru, Z: nas al rahalu)

'Dialogue in the countryside'

(N: 'travelers', Z: 'nomadic people')

N: Salaam takum.

'Peace.'

Z: Salaam takum kamaan. Itakum ja min wen?

'Peace to you also. Where have you come from?'

N: Aniina ja min Juba. Itakum gi geni fi beled de min bedri?

'We came from Juba. Have you been living in this area a long time?'

Z: La', de ma beled taniina. Aniina rahalu beled taniina baiid min ini, u kulu mahaal geriib min bahar de bitaa nas beled de.

'No, this is not our area. We are nomads. Our area is far from here, and the whole place near this river belongs to the people of this area.'

N: Nas del gi zarau shunuu?

'What do these people grow?'

Z: Humon gi zarau dura u basal.

'They grow millet and onions.'

N: Gabiila takum shunuu?

'What tribe are you?'

Z: Gabiila taniina Mundaari. Fi le aniina bagaraat.

'Our tribe is Mundaari. We have cattle.'

N: Aniina ainu nas ma bagaraat hinaak fi jebel. Del min nas takum?

'We saw people with cattle there at the mountain. Are they your people?'

Z: Ai, del min nas taniina. Humon fetishu moya.

'Yes, they are our people. They are looking for water.'

N: Fi mahaal moya geriib min ini? Wala itakum gi jibu min biraat?

'Is there a watering place near here or do you carry water from wells?'

149

Z: Aniina gi jibu min biraat fi wokit ta sef, lakiin fi moya fi koraat hasi de ashaan kariif. Badi matar itakum bi rowa le wen?

'We carry from wells during the summer time, but there is water in the streams now because of rainy season. After the rain where will you go?'

N: Aniina bi rowa le Rajaaf ainu hajaat ta nas gedimiin. Teriig de bi shilu aniina le Rajaaf?

'We will go to Rejaf to see things of the people of old times. Will this trail take us to Rejaf?'

Z: Ai, de teriig ta Rajaaf. Rowa takum adiil geriib min bahar.

'Yes, this is the trail to Rejaf. Go straight along the river.'

Kelimaat ziada al der arufu

1. Some tribes are nomadic, particularly those who own cattle since they must search for water and grass during the dry season.

2. The Mundaari are closely related to the Bari but have kept their cattle, whereas other Bari groups have turned to agriculture.

3. *Beled* may refer to an area or to the land of a particular village.

4. The year is generally divided into two seasons: *sef* 'dry season' and *kariif* 'rainy season'. The latter is also called *zaman ta matar* 'time of rain'.

Kelimaat

bagara (*pl* bagaraat)	'cow'
bagaraat	'cattle'
baiid/boiid	'far'
basal	'onion(s)'
basal (*pl* basalaat)	'onion'
bir (*pl* biraat)	'well' *(n)*
fetishu	'look for'
gaba	'forest, countryside'
gabiila	'tribe'
kariif	'rainy season'
kor (*pl* koraat)	'river, stream, creek bed (dry except during rains)'
matar	'rain'
Mundaari	'Bari subtribe'
rahalu	'nomadic travel'
sef	'summer, dry season'

Asilaat le temriin

1. Itakum gi geni fi Juba min bedri? Min wenu?
2. ta limu ma nas gi rahalu fi gaba?
3. Nas al gi rahalu min gabiila yatuu?
4. Nas fi beled zarau shunuu?
5. Fi le itakum bagaraat?
6. Fi le itakum arabiyaat?
7. Yatuu jebel geriib min Juba?
8. Ita min nas yatuu?
9. Itakum geni fi baga?
10. Moya de gi ja min wen: min bahar wala kor wala bir?
11. Ita ruwa fi gaba ashaan fetishu shunuu?
12. Ita deru moya min bir?
13. Fi matar fi kariif wala fi sef?
14. Ita deru wokit ta sef wala wokit ta kariif?
15. Teriig yatuu bi shilu aniina le Rajaaf?

Deris nimira teletiin
Safar be arabiiya

Lesson 30
Travel by car

Kalaam ta safar be arabiiya
(Y: Yusif, K: Kamaal)

'Dialogue about travel by car'
(Y: Joseph, K: Kamaal)

Y: Itakum bi safiru?

'Are you going to travel?'

K: Ai, aniina bi safiru le Wau badi bukra.

'Yes, we are traveling to Wau the day after tomorrow.'

Y: Itakum bi rowa be arabiiya?

'Will you go by car?'

K: Kan fi tiyaara mara tai bi safiru ma huwa. Kan tiyaara ma fi, huwa bi safiru ma ana be arabiiya. Lakiin huwa ma deru be arabiiya.

'If there is a plane, my wife will go by it. If there isn't a plane, she will travel with me by car. But she does not want to travel by car.'

Y: Kam yom zol bi safiru min Juba le hadi Wau be arabiiya?

'How many days does one travel from Juba to Wau by car?'

K: Kan teriig kweis, bi shilu itiniin yom. Kan teriig bataal, bi shilu telaata wala arba yom.

'If the road is good, it will take two days. If the road is bad, it will take three or four days.'

Y: Kan mara taki safiru ma tiyaara, ita bi safiru baraau?

'If your wife travels by airplane, will you travel alone?'

K: La', fi teriig de zol ma bagder safiru baraau. Kan arabiiya karabu wala kan gilibu wala sedemu, lazim wahid ainu arabiiya u tani bi rowa fetishu nas ashaan ja saaidu.

'No, on that road a person cannot travel alone. If the car breaks down, or if it turns over or crashes, one person must watch the car while the other will go look for people to come help.'

153

Y: Seii, teriig de sab! 'That road is really difficult!'
K: Ai, teriig de sab kalis. Ita bi gatau 'Yes, the road is very difficult. You
sahra u lazim zol bi shilu moya u will cross the desert and a person
akil u benziin ta arabiiya ta telaa- must take water, food, and petrol
ta yom. for the car for three days.'
Y: Shukran, ya sabii. Safiru be ker, 'Thank you, friend. Travel safely,
biduun mushkila. without trouble.'
K: Shukran, u kan Rabuuna saaidu 'Thank you, and if God helps me,
ana, ana gi rowa kweis. I am going well.'

Kelimaat

benziin	'petrol, gasoline'
gatau	'cross'
gediim	'old times'
gilibu	'turn over'
januub	'south'
karabu	'break down'
ker	'well, safe'
safar	'traveling'
sahra	'desert'
sedemu	'crash'
sura	'fast'

Asilaat le temriin

1. Nas munuu bi safiru le Wau u miteen?
2. Mara ta Kamaal deru safiru be shunuu?
3. Kamaal deru safiru be shunuu?
4. Kam yom zol bi safiru min Juba le hadi Wau?
5. De munuu mara to safiru be tiyaara huwa bi safiru be arabiiya?
6. Kam sa zol bi safiru min Juba le hadi Wau be tiyaara? Min Nairobi?
7. Teriig shunuu nas bi gatau sahra u lazim nas bi shilu moya u akilaat u benziin?
8. Kam degiiga zol bi rowa be arabiiya min Juba le hadi Rajaaf?
9. Ita deru gilibu fi arabiiya?
10. Munuu deru gatau sahra be arabiiya gediim?
11. Ita deru gatau sahra be arabiiya wala be tiyaara wala be bas?
12. Le shunuu fi sedemu ketiir fi Juba?
13. Sahra wenu: fi shamaal wala fi januub?
14. Ita sugu arabiiya be ker wala be sura?
15. Fi sahra fi dukaan u benziin? Nas jibu akil u benziin min wen?
16. Fi sahra fi nas ketiir saaidu nas al safiru?

17. Ita deru safiru fi sahra wala fi gaba? Le?
18. Rahalu jibu moya min wen?
19. Kan ita safiru baiid ita deru safiru baraau?
20. Ita durubu haywanaat fi gaba baraau?
21. Fi kura gadam gilibuu nas munuu?
22. Malakia gilibu Kator?

Deris nimira itiniin u teletiin   Lesson 31
Ma zol gi sowru   With the photographer

Kalaam ma zol al gi sowru
(S: Januub Sudaani, K: kawaaja)

'Dialogue with the photographer'
(S: 'South Sudanese', K: 'foreigner')

S: Sabab al kelii ita ja fi Januub Sudaan ini shunuu?

'What reason brought you to South Sudan?'

K: Ana deru sowru sura ta tariik Januub Sudaan. Hasi de ana gi sowru biyuut gedimiin fi Rajaaf. Rajaaf jemiil kalis. Lakiin haja al batal fogo: nas mafi fogo u biyuut jemiliin kasuru.

'I want to take pictures of the history of South Sudan. Now I am photographing old buildings of Rejaf. Rejaf is very pretty. But the bad thing about it is: there are no people in it and the beautiful houses are ruined.'

S: Ita baraau wala ma nas taniin?

'Are you alone or with other people?'

K: Aniina arba: wahid gi sowru fi Konyo Konyo u wahid bahar u wahid tani masuul le aniina. Aniina deru amulu filim.

'We are four: one is photographing Konyo Konyo and another is photographing the river, and the other is our supervisor. We want to make a movie.'

S: Itakum deru amulu shunuu ma filim de?

'What do you want to do with this film?'

K: Aniina deru worii fi tilivizyoon ta beled taniina.

'We want to show it on television of our country.'

S: Ma mumkin aniina bi ainu fi tilivizyoon ta aniina?

'Is it not possible for us to see it on our television?'

K: De hasab nas takum ini fi Januub Sudaan.

'That depends upon your people here in South Sudan.'

S: Hukuuma yauu de gi dafau le itakum guruush le shokol de?

'Does this government pay you money for this work?'

K: Ai, hukuuma ta aniina bi wadii le aniina mohiiya u hukuuma ta Januub Sudaan ini bi wadii arabiiya u nas bi worii teriig.

'Yes, our government will give us a salary and the government of South Sudan will give us cars and people to show the way.'

Kelimaat

awaaru	'show'
filim	'movie'
hukuuma	'government'
kamara	'camera'
karubu	'wasted'
kasuru	'ruined'
masuul	'supervisor'
mohiiya (*pl* mowaahi)	'salary'
sabab	'reason'
sakit	'only, just'
tariik	'history'
tilivizyoon	'television'

Asilaat le temriin

1. Sabab al kelii ita ja fi Januub Sudaan ini shunuu?
2. Ita arifu sowru sura?
3. Ita indu kamara?
4. Ita deru deresu tariik ta Januub Sudaan?
5. Ita deru sowru biyuut gedimiin wala jedidiin, wala ita ma deru sowru biyuut ta kulu kulu?
6. Ita safiru le Rajaaf? Rajaaf wenu?
7. Ita deru alabu fi bahar kebiir dak wala sowru sura sakit?
8. Ita gi ishtaagal baraau wala ma nas taniin?
9. Munuu masuul le ita?
10. Ita deru amulu filim? Ita deru amulu filim ta shunuu?
11. Ita deru amulu shunuu ma filim de?
12. Ita deru worii fi tilivizyoon ta beled takum?
13. Fi Ameerika seii nas bi ainu tilivizyoon kulu yom min sabaa le hadi sa itnaasher?
14. Shunuu hasab nas ini fi Januub Sudaan?
15. Hukuuma gi dafau le ita guruush le shokol taki?
16. Ita gi jibu mohiiya min wen?
17. Kan ita safiru le Nimule, munuu worii teriig le ita?

18. Mohiiya taki fi Januub Sudaan ini ze mohiiya taki fi beled taki?
19. Jesh jibu mohiiya min wen?
20. Sabab al kelii ita derisu Arabi shunuu?
21. Sabab al kelii hukuuma ma dafau mohiiya le ita shunuu?
22. Le shunuu ita ma gi ishtaagal le hukuuma?
23. Nimule u Yei wenu?
24. Bad ma ita sowru sura, mumkin ita bi amulu filim fi Juba?
25. Mumkin ita worii filim fi Juba?
26. Mumkin ita bi ainu tilivizyoon fi Juba? Sa kam mumkin?
27. Ita gi karabu guruush fi Juba?
28. Biyuut gedimiin u jemiliin u kasuru wenu?
29. Haja al bataal fi Rajaaf shunuu?
30. Haja al kweis fi Juba shunuu?

Deris nimira telaata u teletiin Lesson 32
Id Krismas   Christmas

Kalam ta id Krismas

(P: Philip, L: Louis)

'Dialogue about Christmas'

(P: Philip, L: Louis)

P: Yatuu id kebiir kalis fi Januub Sudaan ini?

'Which holiday is the biggest in South Sudan?'

L: Id Krismas yauu de yom kebiir kalis le Mesihiin. Nas bi nedefu biyuut tomon, u biyuu gumashaat le yal tomon sukuriin u alawaat fi bet u kida.

'Christmas is the biggest day for Christians. People will clean their houses, buy clothes for their small children and sweets at home, and so on.'

P: Kam yom bataala ta Krismas?

'How many days vacation at Christmas?'

L: Le Muslimiin bataala telaata yom, u le Mesihiin kamsa yom, u le yal ta medereesa kulu nas bi wodii kamsa yom.

'For Muslims vacation is three days and for Christians five days, and all school children are given five days.'

P: Nas bi ainu ahal tomon ketiir fi wokit ta Krismas?

'Do people see their families often during the Christmas season?'

L: Ai, awal yom ta Krismas fi sabaa nas bi ruwa fi keniisa, badi dak nas taniin bi ruwa dowru fi biyuut ta ahal tomon u nas taniin bi ruwa rihla. Atfaal bamshi min le bet bi dugu ideen bitoomon u sidu bet bi wadii le humon alawaat au kek au asiir.

'Yes, on the first day of Chistmas in the morning people go to church. After that, some go walking to their family's houses and others go on outings. Children go from house to house clapping their hands, and the owners give them candy or cake or fruit juice.'

161

P: Bileel fi yom ta Krismas nas bi am-ulu shunuu?

'On Christmas night what do people do?'

L: Fi nas bi ruwa fi mahaal haflaat u nas taniin bi ruwa alabu nogaara. Nas kulu bi kun moksutiin.

'There are people who go to parties and other people who go dancing to the drums. All the people are happy.'

P: Kweis, shukran. Id fi Januub Su-daan ini kweis kalis.

'Good, thank you. The holiday in South Sudan here is very good.'

L: Shukran kamaan le ita.

'Thank you also.'

Kelimaat ziada al der arufu

Atfaal 'children' is less common than *yal* but is also heard in Juba. Likewise, *bamshi* 'go' can be heard for *bi ruwa* and *au* 'or' for *wala*.

Kelimaat

alaawa (*pl* alawaat)	'candy, sweets'
asiir	'fruit juice'
atfaal	'children'
au	'or'
bamshi	'go'
bataala	'holiday, days off'
dunia	'world'
Faska	'Easter'
hebu	'like, love'
id	'feast, holiday'
kalis	'most'
kek	'cake'
Krismas	'Christmas'
melaad	'birthday'
Mesiihi	'Messiah, Christ'
Mesiihi (*pl* Mesihiin)	'Christian'
moksuut	'happy'
Muslim (*pl* Muslimiin)	'Muslim' *(n)*
nogaara	'drums'
Yesuua	'Jesus'
yomeen	'two days'

Asilaat le temriin

1. Yatuu id kebiir kalis le Mesihiin fi Januub Sudaan ini?
2. Id Krismas kebiir kalis min id Faska?

3. Seii, yom Krismas nas bi kun moksutiin wala la'?
4. Nas bi amulu shunuu fi yom Krismas?
5. Kam yom nas ma bi ruwa le shokol fi ayaam ta Krismas?
6. Seii, nas bi ainu ahal tomon fi yom Krismas?
7. Seii, fi yom Krismas haflaat bi kun ketiir kalis?
8. Ita fi yom Krismas bi kun moksuut?
9. Krismas ta sena al fat yauu kweis kalis min Krismas to gabulu sena al fat?
10. Ita fi yom Krismas bi ruwa keniisa bileel wala fi sabaa?
11. Ita bi biyuu gumashaat le yal taki fi yom Krismas, wala la'?
12. Itakum fi yom Krismas bi wadii alawaat le yal sukeriin?
13. Fi yom Krismas itakum deriin alabu nogaara wala shunuu?
14. Id Krismas kef fi beled takum?
15. Seii, fi yom wahid ita amulu id Krismas fi Januub Sudaan ini? Fi yatuu mahaal fi Januub Sudaan?
16. Yom kam fi shahar Krismas bi bada?
17. Fi yom kam fi shahar weleduu Yesuua al Mesiihi?
18. Yesuua al Mesiihi mutu u gum min mutu u ruwa le wen?
19. Yom melaad taki bi kun fi yatuu shahar u ita bi amulu shunuu fogo?
20. Isim taki ta keniisa munuu?
21. Seii, fi yom wahid ita amulu Krismas ini wala ma nas ahal taki fi beled takum?
22. Ita Muslim wala Mesiihi?
23. Yomeen gabulu Krismas nas bi amulu shunuu fi biyuut?
24. Atfaal bamshi min bet le bet amulu shunuu?
25. Sidu bet bi wadii shunuu le atfaal?
26. Munuu moksuut fi Krismas--nas kebiriin au atfaal?
27. Le shunuu nas bi hebu nas taniin fi Id Krismas?
28. Le shunuu nas bi wadii hajaat le atfaal?
29. Le shunuu Yesuua al Mesiihi weleduu fi dunia?

Deris nimira arba u teletiin Lesson 33
Id ta Muslimiin   The Feast of the Sacrifice

Kalaam fi Id ta Muslimiin

'Dialogue about the Feast of the Sacrifice'

(P: Philip, A: Ahmed)

(P: Philip, A: Ahmad)

P: Yatuu id kebiir le Muslimiin fi Januub Sudaan ini?

'Which festival is biggest for Muslims in South Sudan here?'

A: Huwo Id Dahiiya fi shahar ta hej.

'That is the Festival of Sacrifice in the month of the pilgrimage.

Nas al ruwa le hej humon bi dabaau kurufaat fi Maka.

People who go to the pilgrimage sacrifice sheep at Mecca.

U nas al ma ruwa bi dabaau kurufaat fi bet u bi wadii laham taniin le nas miskiniin.

And people who don't go (to the pilgrimage) sacrifice sheep at home and give some of the meat to poor people.'

P: Seii, humon bi ruwa ainu ahal tomon fi zaman ta Id Dahiiya?

'Do they go visit their families during the Festival of Sacrifice?'

A: Awal yom ta id humon bi geni fi biyuut tomon.

'The first day of the festival they stay at their homes.

Lakiin fi yom nimira itiniin humon bi ruwa ainu ahal tomon.

But the second day they go visit their families.

U kan nas al ruwa fi hej humon rija min hej, humon bi ruwa ainu humon kamaan.

And when the people who have gone on the pilgrimage return, they will go visit them too.'

P: Ana fekiru Id Ramadaan huwa yauu id kebiir.

'I thought that Ramadan was the biggest festival.'

A: Id Ramadaan kamaan kebiir.

'Ramadan is also big.

165

Ita bi ainu Muslimiin humon ma bi akul fi zaman ta Ramadaan min sabaa le hadi sa sita ashiiya.

You will see that Muslims don't eat during Ramadan from morning to six o'clock in the evening.

Bataal kan zol akulu u ashrubu ila bad sa sita ashiiya.

It is bad if a person eats and drinks except after six in the evening.

Bad dak bi kun id, kan shahar ta som kalasu.

After that comes the festival, when the month of the fast is finished.'

P: Shukran, ya Ahmed, ashaan ita worii le ana kalaam ta id ta Muslimiin.

'Thank you, Ahmad, because you explained to me the Muslim festival.'

A: Afwan le ita kamaan. Ma salaam taki.

'You are welcome. Goodbye.'

Kelimaat ziada al der arufu

The *Id Dahiiya* is sometimes known by its Turkish name *Korban Bairam*. It is the biggest festival of the Islamic year and occurs on the 15th of the month of pilgrimage (*haj*). It is forty days after Ramadan. The *Id Fatuur* 'Breakfast Festival' at the end of Ramadan is also known as *Ramadan Bairam*. Both are public holidays in South Sudan.

Kelimaat

hej	'pilgrimage to Mecca'
Id Dahiiya	'Feast of Sacrifice'
Id Fatuur	'Breakfast Feast at the end of Ramadan'
ila	'except'
Maka	'Mecca'
miskiin	'poor, helpless'
nahaar	'daytime'
Ramadaan	'Ramadan'
som	'fast (abstinence from food and water)'
somu	'fast' *(v)*
worii	'explain'

Asilaat le temriin

1. Yatuu id kebiir le Muslimiin fi Januub Sudaan ini?
2. Id Dahiiya awal fi sena wala Id Ramadaan awal?
3. Nas al ruwa le hej humon bi ruwa le wen?
4. Fi Maka humon bi amulu shunuu?
5. Nas al ma ruwa bi amulu shunuu fi bet tomon? U shunuu tani?
6. Nas miskiniin wenu?
7. Nas fi bet bi amulu shunuu fi awal yom?

8. Humon bi amulu shunuu fi yom nimira itiniin?
9. Fi Id Ramadaan nas bi amulu shunuu?
10. Al bataal shunuu fi kulu nahaar fi shahar Ramadaan?
11. Som ta nas Muslimiin kef? Yatuu sa humon ma bi akulu u ashrubu moya?
12. Nihaaya Id Ramadaan id shunuu tani?
13. Ita bi somu? Miteen?
14. Fi beled takum fi som ze som ta Muslimiin?
15. Ita deru ruwa le Maka?
16. Maka wenu?
17. Fi shunuu fi Maka?
18. Ita bagder dabaau kurufaat?
19. Fi kurufaat fi beled takum? Wenu?
20. Kef Id Dahiiya kebiir kalis min Id Ramadaan?
21. Al bataal le ita shunuu fi Januub Sudaan ini?
22. Ita bi somu fi shahar kam fi sena?
23. Nas Muslimiin bi somu kam yom?
24. Mesihiin bi somu kamaan au la'?
25. Yal ta Muslimiin bi somu kamaan ze nas kebiriin?

Deris nimira kamsa u teletiin   Lesson 34
Gisa: Fil Al Bataal Story: The Bad Elephant

[line 1: Arabic; line 2: literal translation; line 3: paraphrase]

Fil   Al   Bataal
Elephant   The   Bad
The Bad Elephant

Kan fi zamaan bedri fi   fil   kebiir u   semiin.
Was at time   early was elephant big   and   fat.
A long time ago there was a big, fat elephant.

Fi yom min ayaam fil   ruwa u   ainu bet ta ter fog ta shejara.
On day from days   elephant went and saw nest of bird top of tree.
One day he went and saw a bird's nest in the top of a tree.

Huwo gum shilu be ida to, juru   teet,   u   gum   dusu
He   arose took by trunk his, pulled down, and arose stomped

    iyaal   ta ter   be kureen to, u   katalu iyaal   ta ter.
    babies of bird by foot   his, and killed babies of bird.
*He took it in his trunk, pulled it down, stomped the baby birds with his foot,
and killed them.*

169

Uma	ta	iyaal	rija	u	arifu	fil	yauu	katalu	iyaal
Mother	of	babies	returned	and	knew	elephant	that	killed	babies

to,	u	gum	kore.
her,	and	arose	cried.

The mother bird returned and knew the elephant had killed her children, and she began to cry.

Min	hinaak	huwo	ruwa	le	fil	u	kelim,	"Ya	fil,	ya
From	there	she	went	to	elephant	and	said,	"Hey	elephant,	hey

semiin,	ya	kebiir,	le	ita	katalu	iyaal	tai	al	sukeriin?"
fat,	hey	big,	why	you	killed	babies	mine	which	small?"

From there she went to the elephant and said, "You big, fat elephant, why did you kill my little babies?"

Fil	gum	zalaan	ma	huwo	wa	sibu	huwo	gi	kore.
Elephant	arose	angry	with	her	and	left	her	-ing	cry.

The elephant became angry with her and left her crying.

Uma	ta	ter	ruwa	le	reyiis	ta	gurabaat	u	gum	worii	le
Mother	of	birds	went	to	chief	of	hawks	and	arose	told	to

huwo	gisa	al	fil	amulu	le	iyaal	to.
him	story	which	elephant	did	to	babies	her.

Then the mother bird went to the chief hawk and told him the story of what the elephant did to her babies.

Gurubaat	ruwa	le	fil	u	bada	dugu	dugu	fil.
Hawks	went	to	elephant	and	began	peck	peck	elephant.

The hawks went to the elephant and began pecking him.

Fil	ainu	ze	de	u	bada	kore,	u	gum	jere,	gi	arfau
Elephant	saw	like	this	and	began	cry,	and	arose	ran,	-ing	raise

adaana	to	kebiir	gi	durubu	kureen	to	fi	wataa.
ears	his	big	-ing	pound	feet	his	on	earth.

The elephant saw that and began crying and running away, flapping his big ears and pounding the earth with his feet.

U   gurabaat lisa ma sibu miskiin   to u   gurabaat gi
And   hawks   still not leave helplessness his and hawks   -ing

    dugu ena to u   ras to.
    peck eyes his and head his.
But the hawks had no pity on him and kept pecking his eyes and his head.

Fil   lisa gi jere u   gi kore.
Elephant still -ing run and -ing cry.
The elephant kept running and crying.

Gurabaat ma ainu miskiin   to u   ma sibu huwo, lisa gi
Hawks   not saw helplessness his and not leave him,   still -ing

    dugu dugu fil,   naman fil   tala amiyaan.
    peck peck elephant, until elephant became blind.
*The hawks still had no pity and would not leave him, but kept on pecking
until he became blind.*

Gowanyaat asma gisa ta fil   al   bataal u al   amiyaan.
Frogs   heard story of elephant which bad   and which blind.
The frogs heard the story of the bad, blind elephant.

Gowanyaat gum ruwa fi hofra kebiir kalis.
Frogs   arose went into hole big   very.
They went to a very big hole.

Humon bada kore fi juwa hofra, "Kok, kok, kok, kok, kok."
They   began cry at inside hole, "Kok, kok, kok, kok, kok."
They began calling from inside the hole, "Kok, kok, kok, kok, kok."

Fil   de huwo tala tabaan u biga   atshaan.
Elephant this he   became tired and became thirsty.
By that time the elephant was very tired and thirsty.

Huwo der   ashrubu moya.
He   wanted drink   water.
He needed a drink of water.

U   wokit huwo asmau gowanyaat gi   kore, huwo   arifu fi
Then when he   heard   frogs   -ing call, he   knew there.was

   moya   fi   mahaal al   gowanyaat gi   kore.
   water   at   place   where frogs   -ing   call.
He heard the frogs croaking and knew there should be water at the place
where they were croaking.

Huwo gum ruwa fi hofra, gum ruwa fogo   huwo gum waga fi
He   arose went to hole, arose went above-it, he   arose fell   into

   hofra, hofra kebiir, u   kasuru adumaat to, u   gum   mutu hinaak.
   hole, hole big,   and broke bones   his, and arose died there.
He went to the hole, right to the top of it, then he fell into that big hole and
broke his bones and he died there.

Mutu ta fil   de   hasil   ashaan   huwo amulu haja   bataal.
Death of elephant this happen because he   did   thing   bad.
So the elephant died because he did a bad thing.

Kelimaat ziada al der arufu

1. Words are occasionally spelled differently to acquaint you with common differences of pronunciation:

   iyaal   instead of yal   'children' (or awlaad or nyerkuuk/nyerkukaat)
   kore   instead of kori   'cry, croak, call (cry of animals)'
   der   instead of deru   'want' (when followed by another verb)

2. Some people prefer *tou* instead of *to* 'his/her', but this spelling leads
   some readers to a strange pronunciation /to.uw/.

3. *Dugu* means 'beat' but was used for 'peck' here. A Bari speaker of Juba
   Arabic would probably have used *togu* 'peck'.

Kelimaat

   adaana   'ears'
   adum (*pl* adumaat)   'bone'
   amiyaan   'blind'
   arfau   'lift, raise'
   atshaan   'thirsty'

bada	'begin a significant continuous event'
dugu	'peck, beat'
dusu	'stomp, stamp'
gani (*pl* ganiaan)	'rich'
gisa	'story'
gony/gowany (*pl* gowanyaat)	'frog'
gum	significant event marker
guraab (*pl* gurabaat)	'hawk, shrike'
hofra	'hole'
ida	'elephant trunk'
jere	'run'
juru	'pull'
katalu	'kill'
miskiin	'helplessness'
naman	'until'
nyerkuuk (*pl* nyerkukaat)	'child'
reyiis/re-iis	'chief'
tabaan	'tired'
tala	'become'
ter	'bird'
togu	'peck'
wataa	'earth, ground'
zalaan	'angry'
zamaan	'a long time ago'

Asilaat le temriin

1. Fil kef: sukeer u jogoot?
2. Fil ainu bet ta shunuu?
3. Bet de wenu?
4. Kef ida ta fil: tawiil wala guseer?
5. Fil juru shunuu min wen?
6. Fil katalu iyaal ta ter kef?
7. Uma ta iyaal kelimu shunuu le fil?
8. Fil amulu shunuu ma ter de?
9. Uma ta ter ruwa le munuu, u amulu shunuu?
10. Munuu dugu dugu fil?
11. Fil amulu shunuu?
12. Adaana ta fil sukeer?
13. Fil durubu kureen to fi shunuu?
14. Gurabaat sibu miskiin ta fil?
15. Gurabaat dugu ena u ras ta fil naman tala kef? U shunuu ta fil?
16. Gowanyaat gi geni wen?

17. Gowany kore kef?
18. Le shunuu fil mutu?
19. Le shunuu nas kelimu gisa de le iyaal tomon?
20. Guraab kef: kebiir wala sukeer?
21. Ita deru dusu iyaal ta ter?
22. Ita deru dusu shunuu?
23. Fi munuu zalaan ma ita?
24. Ita zalaan ma munuu?
25. Ita deru agra gisa? Ita bagder katibu gisa?
26. Adaana taki ze adaana ta fil au ze adaana ta ter?
27. Ita miskiin wala ganiyaan?
28. Munuu tabaan u atshaan?
29. Munuu reyiis ta Januub Sudaan?
30. Shunuu reyiis ta haywanaat?

Glossaries

The number following each gloss indicates the lesson in which the word first occurs. (*Intro* refers to the introduction to this book.) A few very common words are included though they do not occur in the lessons. Some "educated" terms and plurals are included which may not be heard in the countryside. Abbreviations used in the glossaries are: *adj* adjective; *aux* auxiliary; *conj* conjunction; ed. Educated Juba Arabic; *inter* interjection; *n* noun; *pass* passive; *pl* plural; *prep* preposition; *pro* pronoun; *sg* singular; *trans* transitive verb; *v* verb.

Juba Arabic–English

A

abaau forbidden to (14)
abiyad white (21)
abu kind of (9)
abunoo build/built (23)
abuu father (11)
abuuba grandmother (13)
abuuna pastor, priest (24)
abuuy my father (25)
adaana ears (34)
adiil straight (line) (5)
adum (*pl* **adumaat**) bone (34)
afamu understand (10)
afash (*pl* **afashaat**) dish (7)
afashaat luggage, baggage (24)

afeendi (*pl* **afeendiyaat**) official (*n*) (15)
afwan you're welcome (3)
agra read (18)
ahal family (13)
ahlen welcome (*greeting*) (1)
ai yes (1)
ainu see, look (3); see also *shufu*
aj ivory (14)
ajoru (*v*) rent (23); see also *ojora*
aju/auju/azu/auzu want, need (1)
ajuus old (person) (28); see also *gediim*
akbar (*sg* **kabar**) news (13)
akiim doctor (28); see also *diktoor*

175

akil food (6)
akil (*pl* **akilaat**) meal (6)
akir be late (27)
akulu eat/ate (3)
akuu brother (13)
akuu abuu uncle (father's brother) (13)
akwaana brothers and/or sisters (4)
al who/which (6)
al fat last, previous (15)
al jay the next, the coming (16)
Alaa(h) God (25)
alaawa (*pl* **alawaat**) candy, sweets (32)
alabu play (7); dance (24)
alaf/alf one thousand (15)
aleela today (5)
alf/alaf one thousand (15)
alimu understand, learn (3)
Almaania Germany (18)
amalu/amulu make, do (3)
Ameerika America (7)
Ameeriki American (10)
amer red (21)
amiyaan blind (34)
amsiku hold, take (26)
amulu/amalu make, do (3)
amuluu made *(pass)* (3)
ana I/me (1)
andu/indu have (10)
aniina we/us (1)
anwaan address *(n)* (9)
Arabi Arabic (3)
arabiiya (*pl* **arabiyaat**) car (5)
arba four (1)
arbaa see *yom arbaa*
arbataasher fourteen (14)
arbeyiin forty (14)
arfau lift, raise (34)
arifu/arufu know (1)
arkabu get on, ride, climb up (4)
asala question *(v)* (14)

asfar yellow (21)
asha supper (3)
ashaan because (2); in order to (8); for (14)
asha ten (2)
ashiiya late afternoon, evening (27)
ashrib drink! (17)
ashribu/ashrubu drink (3)
asiir fruit juice (32)
asila (*pl* **asilaat**) question *(n)* (2)
asma ita listen please (9); see also *kan ta asma*
asma(u)/asumu hear, listen, obey (2)
aswad black (21)
atfaal children (32)
atshaan thirsty (34)
au or (32)
auju/aju/auzu/azu want, need (1)
awaaru show (31)
awagu injure (28)
awal first, before (14)
awal umbaari day before yesterday (14)
awlaad (*sg* **welid**) children, boys, sons (5)
ayaam (*sg* **yom**) days (5)
ayaan sick (4)
ayaniin sick ones (4)
azu/auzu/aju/auju want, need (1); see also *deru*

B

baar/bahar river, sea (7)
bab (*pl* **babaat**) door, gate (4)
bad ma after (5)
bada(u) begin (5); begin a significant event (34)
badeen/badiin then (5)
bad(i) after (3)
bad(i) shweya in a little while (9)
badiin/badeen then (5)

bagara (*pl* **bagaraat**) cow (29)

bagaraat cows, cattle (29)

bagder can (be able to); know how (10)

bagi remainder (24)

bahar/baar river, sea (7)

baiid/boiid far (29)

bakaan toilet; see also *mustraa*

bamshi go (32); see also *ruwa, mashi*

banaat (*sg* **biniiya**) girls, daughters (10)

bantoloon (pl **bantalonaat**) pants, trousers (11)

bara outside, abroad (4)

baraau alone; on one's own (17)

barid cold (15)

bas (*pl* **basiyaat**) bus (4)

basal (*pl* **basalaat**) onion(s) (29)

bataal bad (1)

bataala holiday, days off (32)

bataatis potato(es) (2)

batariiya (*pl* **batariyaat**) battery (5)

be/bi by, for (1)

be sura (*adj*) fast (30)

bed gidaada chicken egg (1)

bedri early (Intro); long time ago (28)

beled country, village (8)

bembi pink (21)

ben between (14)

benziin petrol, gasoline (30)

beriid al adi surface mail (9)

bes only (8)

besiit easy (11)

bet (*pl* **biyuut**) house, home (3)

bi (*aux*) *future; indefinite* (7)

bi kun will be, will become (13); because (23)

bi/be by, for (1)

biduun without (24)

biga became, got to be (13)

bika mourning (25)

bileel night (23)

biniiya (*pl* **biniyaat/banaat**) girl, daughter (10)

bir (*pl* **biraat**) well (*n*) (29)

bitaa/ta of, belong to (2)

bitaai/tai of me, my, mine (2)

bitaaki/taki of you, your(s) (*sg*) (1)

bitaakum/takum of you, your(s) (*pl*) (1)

bitaniina/taniina of us, our(s) (2)

bitoo(u)/to(u) of him/her/it; his/her(s)/its (2)

bitoomon/tomon of them, their(s) (2)

biyuu buy, sell (11); *see also* for sale

biyuut (*sg* **bet**) houses (5)

bodaboda motorcycle (5)

boiid/baiid far (29)

bordokaal (*n*) orange (12)

Britaanya Britain (7)

budaa cargo, goods (20)

bukra tomorrow (7)

Buluk Buluk District in Juba (23)

bun coffee (3)

busta post (9); see also *maktab busta*

D

daar/dahar (*n*) back (13)

dabaau (*v*) slaughter, sacrifice (26)

dafau pay (9)

dahar/daar (*n*) back (13)

dak that (3)

dakalu/dakulu enter (3); cause to enter; put into (9)

dar riyaada stadium (16)

dasta dozen (2)

Dauud David (9)

dawa (*pl* **dawaat**) medicine (26)

de this (1)

def (*pl* **diyuuf**) guest, visitor (5) (ed.); see also *defaan*

defaan (*pl* **defanaat**) guest,
     visitor (3); see also *def*
degaayg (*sg* **degiiga**) minutes (9)
degiig flour (1)
degiiga (*pl* **degaayg**) minute,
     wait a minute (9)
del these (10)
deriin want (1) (ed. *pl* of *deru*)
deris (*pl* **derisiaat**) lesson (1)
derisu/deresu study (3); teach (8)
deru want, need (1); see also *azu,*
     deriin
dib center (football player) (16)
digin beard (9)
diktoor doctor (25); see also *akiim*
disinteerio dysentery (28)
diyuuf (*sg* **def**) guests, visitors (5);
     see also *defaan*
dofunu bury (26)
dolaab cupboard (15)
dom blood (26)
dor time, turn (14)
dor wahid/wahid dor once, one
     time, one turn (14)
dowriiya *(n)* walk (12)
dowru *(v)* walk (12)
dugu knock, hit, clap (4); peck,
     beat (34)
dukaan (*pl* **dukanaat**) shop,
     store (1)
dunia world (32)
dura millet, sorghum, grain (1)
durubu/udrubu *(v)* phone, call,
     ring (a bell), beat, pound (20);
     hunt, shoot (14)
dusu *(trans)* stamp, stomp, hide
     (34)

E

ena (*pl* **uyuun**) eye (28)
esh bread (1)
esmiinti cement floor (15)

F

faam/faham charcoal (22)
fadal please *(invitation)* (3)
fadi free, empty (6)
faham/faam charcoal (22)
Faraansa France (17)
Faraansi French (10)
Faska Easter (32)
fat see *al fat*
fata(u) open (4)
fatuur breakfast (3); see also *Id Fatuur*
fawaaki fruit (2); fruit trees (12)
fekiru think (4); see also *mata fekiru*
fetishu look for (29)
fi *(prep)* in, at, to (2)
fi *(v)* there is/are; have; possess;
     exist (1)
fil (*pl* **filaat**) elephant (14)
filim movie (31)
fog up, above (7)
fogo in it; on it; above it (15)
form form (18); see also *worniik*
ful peanuts, groundnuts (2)
fustaan (*pl* **fustanaat**) dress (11)

G

gaba forest, countryside (29)
gabiila tribe (29)
gabulu over (11); before (20)
gada lunch/dinner (early
     afternoon) (3)
gadam foot (16)
galam (*pl* **galamaat**) pen, pencil (7)
galtaan guilty (26)
game' wheat (1)
ganamooya (*pl* **ganamoyaat**)
     goat (26)
garb west (Intro)
garbiiya western (18)
gatau cut (7); cross (30)
ge/gi *progressive* (4)
gediim old (thing) (11); old times
     (29); see also *ajuus*

gediiya trial (at court) (26)
geiru *(v)* change (5)
gemiis (*pl* gemisiyaat) shirt (11)
geni sit down (3); live, stay (4)
geriib (ma) near (to) (4); about to (5); recent (8)
gi/ge *progressive* (4)
gibeel already (3)
gidaam ahead (5)
gilibu defeat (16); turn over (30)
gilibuu defeated (16)
girid (*pl* guruud) monkey (14)
gisa story (34)
gisim body, health (13)
gofulu/gofolu shut, close (4)
gon goal (16)
gony/gowany (*pl* gowanyaat) frog (34)
gowi dried up, hard (21)
gufa (*pl* gufaat) basket (2)
gum *(conj) significant event marker* (34)
gum *(v)* take off, get up, wake up, arise (27)
gumaash (*pl* gumashaat) cloth, material, clothes (11)
gumaash fi juwa lining (19)
guraab (*pl* gurabaat) hawk, shrike (34)
guruud (*sg* girid) monkeys (15)
guruush money (1)
guseer short (12)

H

habuub wind, storm (Intro)
hafla (*pl* haflaat) party (17)
haja (*pl* hajaat) thing (1)
hamaam bathroom (22)
hamim bathe (12)
hasab according to (7)
hasi de now, just (4)
hasil happen (26)
hawa air (23)

hawe around, surrounding (17)
hay district (23)
haywaan (*pl* haywanaat) animal (14)
hebu like, love (32)
hej pilgrimage to Mecca (33)
hejiz reservation (27)
helu sweet, pretty (12)
hidaasher eleven (6)
hinaak there (12)
Hindi Hindu (10)
hisa class (10)
hofra hole (34)
hukuuma government (31)
huma *(n)* cold (illness) (28)
humon they/them (1)
huwo he/him; she/her; it (1)

I

id feast, holiday (32)
Id Dahiiya Feast of Sacrifice (33)
Id Fatuur Breakfast Feast at end of Ramadan (33)
ida (*pl* ideen) hand, arm, handle (19); elephant trunk (34)
ideen (*sg* ida) hands (4)
ikwaat (*sg* okot) sisters (13)
ila less, minus (6); except (33)
indana we have (ed.) (13)
indi I have (ed.) (13)
indu/andu have (10)
indum they have (ed.) (13)
Ingliizi English (10)
iris wedding (24); see also *zowiju*
isheriif maize, corn (1)
ishriin twenty (8)
ishtaagal *(v)* work (11)
isim name (17)
istiidiu studio (24)
ita you *(sg)* (1)
itakum you *(pl)* (1)
itiniin/itniin two (1)
itiniin/itniin dor twice (14)

itnaasher twelve (6)
itniin/itiniin two (1)
itniin/itiniin dor twice (14)
iyaal/yal children (4)
izin taki excuse me (8)

J

ja come/came (3)
ja-aan/jaan hungry (7)
jahiz ready, made (11)
jalabiiya jalabiya (11)
jama university (5)
januub south (30)
Januub Sudaan South Sudan (5)
Januub Sudaani (*pl* **Januub Sudaniin**) South Sudanese (*n*) (8)
jarasoon (*pl* **jarasonaat**) waiter (6)
jawaab (*pl* **jawabaat**) letter (9); answer (10)
jawaab al gi ruwa be tiyaara airform, air letter (9)
jawabu (*v*) reply, answer (10)
jay next, coming (with al) (16)
jaz gas (22)
jaz abiyad kerosine, paraffin (22)
jebel hill, mountain (12)
jediid new (11)
jemiil beautiful, pretty (12)
jena (*pl* **yal**) child (7)
jenaa wing (football player) (16)
jeraan (*pl* **jeranaat**) neighbor (8)
jere run (34)
jeribu taste (22)
jeriida magazine (22)
jesh army (17)
jeziira (*pl* **jeziraat**) island (12)
jibna cheese (19)
jibu bring, hand, give (1)
jibuu was brought (8)
jidi grandfather (13)
jilid leather, skin (19)

jinee pound (SSP=South Sudanese Pound) (1)
jineena (*pl* **jinenaat**) garden (12)
jinis nationality (18)
jo weather
jogoot thin, skinny (12)
juluus parlor, living room (7)
juru pull (34)
juwa inside (12)
juwa (*pl* **juwaat**) house, inside place (15)
juwa motbak; motbak kitchen (15)
juwa ta arabiiya carport (lit. inside place for cars)

K

kabaab beef kabob (6)
kabar (*pl* **akbar**) news (13)
kadaam (*pl* **kadamaat/ kadamiin**) house worker (4)
kafaara sympathy (13)
kafiif light (weight) (11)
kafu (min) afraid (of) (14)
Kahira Cairo (27)
kahraba electricity (22)
kal uncle (mother's brother) (13)
kalaam talk, dialogue (1); matter, case (26)
kalaas finished, okay (1)
kalasu finish (1)
kalis very (2); most (32)
kalti aunt (mother's sister) (13)
kam how much/many (1)
kamaan also (1)
kamara camera (31)
kamastaasher fifteen (15)
kamsa/kamiisa five (2)
kamsiin fifty (14)
kan (*conj*) if, when (5)
kan (*v*) was (5)
kan ita asma/kan ta asma please; if you will (10)
kaniisa church (24)

karabu ruined (5); break down (30)

kariif rainy season (29)

kasiil clothes-washing (1)

kaslaan lazy (22)

kasulu wash (7)

kasuru broken (not glass) 15); (ruined (31)

katalu kill (34)

katib clerk (9)

katibu write/wrote (7)

kawaaja (*pl* **kawajaat**) foreigner (8)

kayaata sewing (11); see also *keitu*

kebiir big, large (9)

kef how (4)

keitu sew (11); see also *kayaata*

kek cake (32)

kelii may (8); let (9); cause (24)

kelima (*pl* **kelimaat**) word (1)

kelimu say, tell (7)

keniisa/kaniisa church (24)

ker (*adj*) well, safe (30)

keshifu examine (25)

ketiir (too) much/many (2)

kibda (*pl* **kibdaat**) liver (6)

kida u kida so-so (16); see also *u kida*

kilo kilo (2)

kis (*pl* **kisiaat**) bag (1)

kitaab (*pl* **kitabaat**) book (22)

kokoora redivision (Intro)

kom pile (2)

komsomiiya five hundred (15)

kor (*pl* **koraat**) river, stream, creek bed (dry except during rains) (29)

kori/kore cry, mourn (25)

kori-kori argue (26)

koroofo greens (2)

kortoon cardboard box (15)

kot coat (24)

Krismas Christmas (32)

kubaaya (*pl* **kubayaat**) cup, glass (5)

kubri bridge (12)

kubu pour (21)

kudru/kudra (*pl* **kudruwaat**) a leafy green vegetable (11)

kulu all, every (2); altogether (6); see also *ta kulu ku*

kuluub restaurant (6)

kura ball (16)

kureen leg, foot (28)

kursi (*pl* **kursiyaat**) chair (11)

kuruuf (*pl* **kurufaat**) sheep (26)

kutu put (22)

kweis(a)/kwesii (*pl* **kweisiin**) good, well, okay (1)

L

la' no (1)

laam/laham meat (1)

lahib player (16)

lakiin but (3)

lazim of course, certainly (8); must, have to (9)

le to (1); why? (15); see also *le shunuu*

le ana to me (17); see also *lei*

le anu because (19)

le hadi/li hadi until (5)

le shunuu why? (15); see also *le*

leben milk (Intro)

lei to me (17); see also *le ana*

lemuun lemon(s) (2); lemonade (3); lime(s) (12)

leyin soft (22)

li hadi/le hadi until (5)

libisu put on, wear (24)

lifu turn (5); circle around (24); wrap (28); see also *robutu*

ligoo meet (14); find, discover (26)

limu meet (8)

lisa still, not yet (3)

lon (*pl* **lonaat**) color (11)

lori lorry, truck (4)

M

ma not (1)
ma ana; mai with me (17)
ma humon; moom with them (17)
ma huwo; moo with him (17)
ma kweis not good (bad) (11)
maa with (1)
maal (*pl* malaat); mahaal (*pl* mahalaat) place (2)
maasalaam taki/takum goodbye (lit. with your peace *sg/pl*) (1)
magaas scissors (22)
magisu reduce, discount (2)
mahaal (*pl* mahalaat); maal (*pl* malaat) place (2)
mai; ma ana with me (17)
Maka Mecca (33)
makana (*pl* makanaat) engine (5); machine, sewing machine (11)
makaniiki mechanic (8)
maktab (*pl* maktabaat) office (5)
maktab busta post office (9)
mala fill in (18)
malaaria malaria (28)
malaga spoon (22)
maleesh sorry, never mind (5)
maliiya finance (20)
mama mama, mommy (7)
mana meaning (10)
manga mango(es) (2)
manga (*pl* mangaat) mango (2)
mara (*pl* mariaat) woman, wife (3)
martaba mattress, bed (22)
maruwaa/muruwaa fan (for cooling air) (23)
mashaakil (*sg* mushkila) troubles, problems (24)
masi/mashi go/went (2)
Masir Egypt (11)
masuul supervisor (31)
masuura water tap (23)
mata (*pl* matakum) don't (4)

mata fekiru never mind (4)
mataar(a) airport (27)
matar rain (29)
medreesa/medereesa school (3)
Mesiihi Messiah, Christ (32)
Mesiihi (*pl* Mesihiin) Christian (32)
mile salt (1)
milyoon one million (15)
min from (3)
miskiin poor, helpless (33); helplessness (34)
miteen (*adj*) two hundred (15)
miteen (*inter*) when (7)
miya one hundred (14)
mofugu break out in rash (26)
mohiiya (*pl* mowaahi) salary (31)
moksuut happy (32)
mokwa iron, ironing (15)
moo with him/her/it (17)
moom with them (17)
moshruu' project (20)
motbak/juwa motbak kitchen (15)
mowaahi (*sg* mohiiya) salary (31)
moya water (3)
moya lemuun lemonade (3)
mubaraa match, game (16)
muda period of time (3)
mudeeris (*pl* muderisiin/muderisiat) teacher (5)
muftaa (*pl* muftahaat) key (9)
mugshaash(a) broom (22)
muhaamur fried (6)
muhaandis engineer (17)
mukaayif hawa evaporation cooler (23)
mulaa(h) stew, sauce (22)
mumkin possible (9)
munaazama organization (18)
Mundaari Bari sub-tribe (29)
munuu who(m)? (11)
muraaja review (10)
murkab boat (12)

muruwaa/maruwaa fan (for cooling air) (23)

mushkila (*pl* **mashaakil**) trouble, problem (24)

Muslim (*pl* **Muslimiin**) Muslim (*n*) (32)

mustraa toilet (23); see also *bakaan*

musu/muze not (11)

musu/muze kweis isn't it good? (11)

muta-akir (*adj*)

muteeheda late (27) united (8); see also *Umam al Muteeheda*

mutu die, death (13)

muwaazif employee, worker, official (8)

muze/musu not (11)

muze (de)? isn't that so? (6)

N

nadii call (19)

nagisu reduce, discount (2)

nahaar daytime (33)

nahaar de today (5)

naman until (34)

nas (*sg* **zol**) people (12)

nedifu clean (15)

nenzil/nezil get down (14)

ni-/no- told me to (22)

nihaaya end (16); finally, lastly (18)

nimira (*pl* **nimiraat**) number (1)

no-/ni- told me to (22)

nogaara drums (32)

nota notebook (18)

num sleep (10)

nus half (2)

nus nus half and half (10)

nyerkuuk (*pl* **nyerkukaat**) child (34)

O

oda (*pl* **odaat**) room (3)

oda juluus parlor, living room (7)

oda num bedroom (15)

ojora (*n*) rent (23); see also *ta ojora* and *ajoru*

okot/ukut (*pl* **ikwaat**) sister (13)

okot abuu aunt (father's sister) (13)

orbomiiya four hundred (15)

osh compound, yard (5)

P

pasport passport (18)

R

rabaat/robaat wrapping, bandage (28)

Rabuuna Lord (8)

radio radio (10)

rahalu nomadic travel (29)

rajil (*pl* **rujaliin**) man (2)

rakabu cook (22)

Ramadaan Ramadan (33)

ras head (28)

rasulu send (9)

re-iis/reyiis chief (34)

resemu/resimu draw, embroider (11)

resim embroidery (11)

reyiis/re-iis chief (34)

rihla outing (14)

rija return (4)

robaat/rabaat wrapping, bandage (28)

robutu wrap (28); see also *lifu*

roksa/ruksa license (14)

rotaan language (Intro)

rowa/ruwa go/went (2)

rubu one fourth (6)

rudu we've agreed (11)

rujaliin (*sg* **rajil**) men (2)

ruksa/roksa license (14)

ruwa/rowa go/went (2)

ruz rice (1)

S

sa (*pl* **sa-aat**) hour, watch (4)

saab/sab difficult, hard (11)
saaidu *(v)* help (8)
saar/shahar month (Intro)
sab/saab difficult, hard (11)
saba seven (2)
sabaa morning (10)
sabab reason (31)
sabataasher seventeen (17)
sabi sir (6)
sabii friend (14)
sabuun soap (1)
safa (*pl* **safaat**) section, line,
    queue (9)
safar traveling (30)
safiru travel (4)
sah right, correct (10)
sahil easy (11); see also *besiit*
sahra desert (30)
sakanu warm up (16)
sakit only, just (31)
sala bald (9)
sala/salau repair (5)
salaa (*pl* **salawaat**) prayer (24)
salaam hello (lit. peace) (1)
salaam taki hello (lit. peace to
    you, *sg*) (1)
salaam takum hello (lit. peace to
    you, *pl*) (1)
salamaat hello *(sg)* (1)
salamaatkum hello *(pl)* (1)
salata salad (6)
salau/sala repair (5)
samaga fish (2)
sawaag (*pl* **sawagiin**) driver (5)
sebeyiin seventy (14)
sebit; yom sebit Saturday (16)
sedemu crash (30)
sef summer, dry season (29)
seii is it true that...? (5)
sejilu register (9); score (16)
selemu collect (9)
seli pray (24)
semiin fat (12)

sena year (8)
senduuk (*pl* **sendukaat**) box (9)
seriir bed frame (23)
shaar/shahar hair (22)
shagaal worker (8)
shahar/saar (*pl* **shuhuur**) month (3)
shamaal left, north (5)
shanta bag, case (19)
shargiiya eastern (18)
sharia street (8); see also *teriig*
shatir clever, intelligent (7)
shay tea (1)
shediid very (6)
shejara (*pl* **shejaraat**) tree, shrub (21)
sherika company (17)
shikil shape, kind (21)
shilu take (14)
shokol *(n)* work (8)
shot half (of a football game) (16)
shubaak (*pl* **shubakaat**) window
    (15)
shufu see, look (3); see also *ainu*
shuhuur (*sg* **shahar**) months (3)
shukran/sukuran thank you (1)
shunuu what? (1)
shurba soup (6)
shweya a little (2)
sibu leave (19)
sid owner, keeper (1)
sifir zero (16)
sikiin knife (22)
sikirteer secretary (8)
siniin sharp (22)
siniiya roundabout (5)
sita six (2)
sitaasher sixteen (16)
sitiin sixty (14)
sobuura blackboard (10)
som fast (abstinence from food
    and water) (33)
somu *(v)* fast (33)
sowru take pictures (12)
subumiiya seven hundred (15)

sugu drive (14)
suk (*pl* **sukaat**) market (2)
sukeer small (11)
sukun hot (15)
sukur sugar (1)
sunuun (*pl* **sununaat**) tusk (14)
sura (*pl* **suraat**) picture (11)
sutumiiya six hundred (15)

T

ta/bitaa of, belong to (2)
ta biyuu for sale (21)
ta kulu kulu at all (5)
ta ojora for rent (23)
taal/ta-aal come! (3)
tabaan tired (34)
tabau *(v)* type (20)
tabe (*pl* **tawaabe**) stamp (9)
tai/bitaai of me, my, mine (2)
takalu *(v)* work (11); see also
    ishtaagal
taki/bitaaki of you, your(s) *(sg)* (1)
takum/bitaakum of you, your(s)
    (pl) (1)
tala go out, go over, exceed (9);
    become (34)
tala gowi wither, dry up (21)
talaaja refrigerator (22)
talaata/telaata three (2)
talab order, request (Intro)
talataasher thirteen (13)
taliba (*pl* **talibaat**) student (10)
tamaanya eight (2)
taman *(n)* price (19)
tamaniin eighty (14)
tamantaasher eighteen (18)
tani else, other (1); again (10)
taniin others (1); some (32)
taniina/bitaniina of us, our(s) (2)
tariik history (31)
taskar(a) ticket (27)
tawaabe (*sg* **tabe**) stamps (9)
tawaali straight (Intro)

tawiil long, tall (11)
teb okay (9)
teet/tehet down, below, under (7)
tegiil heavy, thick (11)
tehet/teet down, below, under (7)
teksi taxi (Intro)
telaata/talaata three (2)
telefoon telephone (20)
teletiin thirty (14)
telij ice (22)
temriin drills (2)
ter bird (34)
terebeeza (*pl* **terebezaat**) table (5)
teriig road, way (5); see also *sharia*
tilit one third (6)
tilivizyoon television (31)
tilmiis pupil, student (Intro)
tisa nine (2)
tisataasher nineteen (19)
tiseyiin ninety (14)
tiyaara (*pl* **tiyaraat**) airplane (9)
to(u)/bitoo(u) of him/her/it;
    his/her(s)/its (2)
togu peck (34); see also *dugu*
tomon/bitoomon of them, their(s) (2)
tumunumiiya/tumonmiiya eight
    hundred (15)
turaab dust, dirt (15)
tusomiiya nine hundred (15)
tuwaliin *(pl)* long, tall (11); see *tawiil*

U

u/wa and (2)
u kida etc., and so on (10)
udrubu/durubu *(v)* phone, call,
    ring (a bell), beat, pound (20);
    hunt, shoot (14)
ukut/okot sister (13)
uma (*pl* **umahaat**) mother (7)
umaar donkey (Intro)
umam nations (8)
Umam al Muteeheda United
    Nations (8)

umbaari yesterday (4)
usbuu week (7)
uyuun (*sg* **ena**) eyes (28)

W

wa/u and (2)
wadii/wodii give, take, lend to (19)
waga fall/fell (28)
wagif(u)/woguful stop, stand (4)
wahid/waid one (1); same (9)
wahid dor/dor wahid once, one
    time, one turn (14)
waja pain, ache (13)
wala or (3)
wara behind (5)
waraga (*pl* **waragaat**) paper
    (*n*) (6)
waraga ta akilaat
wataa menu (6)
waziifa earth, ground (34)
wazin occupation (18) weight (9)
weled/welid/woled (*pl* **awlaad**)
    boy, son, child (2)
weledu/welidu give birth (7)
weleduu/weliduu born (8)
wen/wenu where? (3)
wizaara ministry (20)
wodii/wadii give, take, lend (19)
woduru lose/lost (9); be (13)
wogufu/wagif(u) stop, stand (14)
wokit time, occasion (8); period of
    time (13)
woled/weled/welid/ (*pl* **awlaad**)
    boy, son, child (2)
worii show (23); explain (33)
worniik form (18); see also *form*
woroma swelling (28)
woromu swell (28)
wunusu converse (10)
wusulu connect (20)

Y

ya *vocative* (2)

ya salaam good heavens! (8)
yal/iyaal (*sg* **jena**) children (4)
yala hey (5); until (26)
yamiin right (nor left) (5)
yani that means (6); that is to say;
    i.e. (18)
yatuu which (23)
yauu specifically (6); self *(after
    pro)* (11)
yauu de here is (2); this one here
    (11)
Yesuua Jesus (32)
yom (*pl* **ayaam**) day (5)
yom arbaa Wednesday (16)
yom itniini Monday (15)
yom juma Friday (16)
yom kamiis Thursday (16)
yom lahad Sunday (16)
yom salasaa/talataa Tuesday (16)
yom sebit; sebit Saturday
yom talataa/salasaa Tuesday (16)
yomeen two days (32)

Z

zabuun (*pl* **zabunaat**) customer (1)
zalaan angry (34)
zalat asphalt (5)
zamaan a long time ago (34)
zaman period of time (13)
zaraaf giraffe (14)
zarau grow, plant (21)
zatu this very *(emphasis)* (8)
ze like, as (21)
zekiru memorize (10)
zerif (*pl* **zeruuf**) envelope (5)
zerif al kebiir parcel, large
    envelope (9)
zeruuf (*sg* **zerif**) envelopes (5)
zet oil (1)
ziada more (1)
ziraa agriculture (18)
ziyaara visit, outing (12)
zol (*pl* **nas**) person (3)

zol indu fikra expert, specialist (18)
zowiju marry (10); see also *iris*

zowijuu married *(pass)* (10)
zuhuur flower, plant (21)

English–Juba Arabic

A

a little shweya (2)
a long time ago zamaan (34); bedri (28)
about to geriib (ma) (5)
above, up fog (7)
above it fogo (15)
abroad bara (4)
according to hasab (7)
ache waja (13)
address *(n)* anwaan (9)
afraid (of) kafu (min) (14)
after bad(i) (3); bad ma (5)
afternoon *see* late afternoon/ evening
again tani (10)
agriculture ziraa (18)
ahead gidaam (5)
air hawa (23)
airform, air letter jawaab al gi ruwa be tiyaara (9)
airplane tiyaara (*pl* tiyaraat) (9)
airport mataar(a) (27)
all kulu (2)
alone baraau (17)
already gibeel (3)
also kamaan (1)
altogether kulu (6)
America Ameerika (7)
American Ameeriki (10)
and u/wa (2)
and so on; etc. u kida (10)
angry zalaan (34)
animal haywaan (*pl* haywanaat) (14)
answer, letter *(n)* jawaab (*pl* jawabaat) (10)
answer, reply *(v)* jawabu (10)

Arabic Arabi (3)
argue kori-kori (26)
arise gum (27)
arm, hand, handle ida (*pl* ideen) (4)
army jesh (7)
around, surrounding hawe (17)
as, like ze (21)
asphalt zalat (5)
at fi (2)
at all ta kulu kulu (5)
ate/eat akulu (3)
aunt (father's sister) okot abuu (13)
aunt (mother's sister) kalti (13)

B

back naar/dahar) (13)
bad bataal (1)
bag kis (*pl* kisiaat) (1)
bag, case shanta (19)
baggage afashaat (24)
bald sala (9)
ball kura (16)
bandage, wrapping rabaat/robaat (28)
Bari sub-tribe Mundaari (29)
basket gufa (*pl* gufaat) (2)
bathe hamim (2)
bathroom hamaam (22)
battery batariiya (*pl* batariyaat) (5)
be woduru (13)
be able to bagder (10)
be late *(v)* akir (27); *see also* late
beard digin (9)
beat, peck dugu (34), togu (34)
beat, pound durubu/udrubu (20)
beautiful, pretty jemiil (12)

became, got to be biga (13); tala (34); see also *will become*

because ashaan (2); le anu (ed.) (19); bi kun (23)

bed, mattress martaba (22)

bed frame seriir (23)

bedroom oda num (15)

beef kabob kabaab (5)

before awal (14); gabulu (20)

begin bada(u) (5)

begin a significant event bada(u) (35)

behind wara (5)

belong to, of ta/bitaa (2)

below, down, under teet/tehet (7)

between ben (14)

big, large kebiir (9)

bird ter (34)

black aswad (21)

blackboard sobuura (10)

blind amiyaan (34)

blood dom (26)

boat murkab (12)

body, health gisim (13)

bone adum (*pl* adumaat) (34)

book kitaab (*pl* kitabaat) (22)

born weleduu/weliduu (8)

box senduuk (*pl* sendukaat) (9)

boy, son, child weled/welid/ woled (*pl* awlaad) (2)

bread esh (1)

break down karabu (30)

break out in a rash mofugu (26)

breakfast fatuur (3)

Breakfast Feast at end of Ramadan Id Fatuur (33)

bridge kubri (12)

bring, hand, give jibu (1)

Britain Britaanya (7)

broken (not glass) kasuru (15)

broom mugshaash(a) (22)

brother akuu (13) (*pl* akwaana) (4)

brothers and/or sisters akwaana (4)

build/built abunoo (23)

Buluk Buluk District in Juba (23)

bury dofunu (26)

bus bas (*pl* basiyaat) (4)

but lakiin (3)

buy, sell biyuu (11)

by, for be/bi (1)

C

Cairo Kahira (27)

cake kek (32)

call nadii (19)

call, phone durubu, udrubu (20)

came/come ja (3)

camera kamara (31)

can (be able to) bagder (10)

candy, sweets alaawa (*pl* alawaat) (33)

car arabiiya (*pl* arabiyaat) (5)

cardboard box kortoon (15)

cargo, goods budaa (20)

carport (lit. **inside place for cars**) juwa ta arabiiya (23)

case, bag shanta (19)

case, matter kalaam (26)

cattle, cows bagaraat (29)

cause *(v)* kelii (24)

cause to enter, put into dakalu/ dakulu (9)

cement floor esmiinti (15)

center (football player) dib (16)

certainly, of course lazim (9)

chair kursi (*pl* kursiyaat) (11)

change *(v)* geiru (5)

charcoal faam/faham (22)

cheese jibna (19)

chicken egg bed gidaada (1)

chief re-iis (34)

child jena (*pl* yal) (7); nyerkuu (*pl* nyerkukaat) (34)

child, boy, son weled/welid/ woled (*pl* awlaad) (2)

children yal/iyaal (4); nyerkukaat (34); atfaal (ed.) (3); awlaad (5)

Christ, Messiah Mesiihi (32)

Christian Mesiihi (*pl* Mesihiin) (32)
Christmas Krismas (32)
church keniisa/kaniisa (24)
circle, turn lifu (28)
clap, knock, hit dugu (4)
class hisa (10)
clean nedifu (15)
clerk katib (9)
clever, intelligent shatir (7)
climb up, get on, ride arkabu (4)
close, shut *(v)* gofolu/gofulu (4)
cloth, clothes, material gumaash
(*pl* gumashaat) (11)
clothes-washing kasiil (1)
coal faam/faham (22)
coat kot (24)
coffee bun (3)
cold *(adj)* barid (15)
cold *(n)* **(illness)** huma (28)
collect selemu (9)
color lon (*pl* lonaat) (11)
come/came ja (3)
come! taal/ta-aal (3)
coming, next al jay (16)
company sherika (17)
compound, yard osh (5)
connect wusulu (20)
converse wunusu (10)
cook rakabu (22)
cooler mukaayif hawa (23)
corn, maize isheriif (1)
correct, right sah (10)
country, village beled (8)
countryside, forest gaba (29)
cow bagara (*pl* bagaraat) (29)
crash *(v)* sedemu (30)
creek bed, stream, riverkor (*pl*
koraat) (29)
cross *(v)* gatau (30)
cry, mourn kori/kore (25)
cup (of glass)kubaaya (*pl*
kubayaat) (5)
cupboard dolaab (15)

customer zabuun (*pl* zabunaat)
(1)
cut gatau (7)

D

dance, play alabu (24)
daughter biniiya (*pl* biniyaat/
banaat) (10)
David Dauud (9)
day yom (5)
day before yesterday awal
umbaari (14)
days ayaam (5)
days off, holiday bataala (32)
daytime naar/nahaar (33)
death, die mutu (13)
defeat gilibu (30)
defeated gilibuu (16)
desert sahra (30)
dialogue, talk *(n)* kalaam (26)
die, death mutu (13)
difficult, hard sab (11)
dinner/ lunch (early afternoon)
gada (3)
dirt, dust turaab (15)
discount *(v);* **reduce** nagisu (2)
discover, find ligoo (26)
dish afash (*pl* afashaat) (7)
district hay (23)
district in Juba Buluk (23)
do, make amulu/amalu (3)
doctor akiim (28); diktoor (25)
donkey umaar (Intro)
don't mata *(sg)* (4); matakum *(pl)* (6)
door, gate bab (*pl* babaat) (4)
down, below, under teet/tehet (7)
dozen dasta (2)
draw, embroider resemu/resimu
(11)
dress fustaan (*pl* fustanaat) (11)
dried up, hard gowi (21)
drills temriin (2)
drink ashribu/ashrubu (3)
drink! ashrib! (17)

drive sugu (14)
driver sawaag (*pl* sawagiin) (5)
drums nogaara (32)
drive sugu (14)
driver sawaag (*pl* sawagiin) (5)
drums nogaara (32)
dry season, summer sef (29)
dry up, wither tala gowi (21)
dust, dirt turaab (15)
dysentery disinteerio (28)

E
early bedri (Intro)
ears adaana (34)
earth, ground wataa (34)
Easter Faska (32)
eastern shargiiya (18)
easy sahil/besiit (11)
eat/ate akulu (3)
egg of a chicken bed gidaada (1)
Egypt Masir (11)
eight tamaanya (2)
eight hundred tumunumiiya (15)
eighteen tamantaasher (18)
eighty tamaniin (14)
electricity kahraba (22)
elephant fil (*pl* filaat) (14)
elephant trunk ida (34)
eleven hidaasher (6)
else tani (1)
embroidery resim (11)
employee, official, office worker muwaazif (8)
empty, free fadi (6)
end nihaaya (16)
engine makana (*pl* makanaat) (5)
engineer muhaandis (17)
English Ingliizi (10)
enter dakalu/dakulu (9)
envelope zerif (*pl* zeruuf) (5)
etc.; and so on u kida (10)
evaporative cooler mukaayif hawa (23)

evening *see* late afternoon
every, all kulu (2)
examine keshifu (25)
exceed, go over tala (9)
except ila (33)
excuse me izin taki (8)
exist; there is/are fi (1)
expert, specialist zol indu fikra (18)
explain worii (33)
eye ena (*pl* uyuun) (28)

F
fall/fell waga (28)
family ahal (13)
fan maruwaa/muruwaa (23)
far baiid/boiid (29)
fast *(adj)* be sura (30)
fast *(n)* som (33)
fast *(v)* somu (33)
fat semiin (12)
father abuu (11)
father's brother (uncle) akuu abuu (13)
father's sister (aunt) okot buui (13)
feast, holiday id (32)
Feast of Sacrifice Id Dahiiya (33)
fifteen kamastaasher (15)
fifty kamsiin (14)
fill in mala (18)
film, movie filim (32)
finally nihaaya (18)
finance maliiya (20)
find, discover ligoo (26)
finish *(v)* kalasu (1)
finished, okay kalaas (1)
first awal (14)
fish samaga (2)
five kamsa/kamiisa (2)
five hundred komsomiiya (15)
flour degiig (1)
flower, plant zuhuur (21)
food akil (6)

foot gadam (16), kureen (28)
football player (center) dib (16)
football player (wing) jenaa (16)
for ashaan (14)
for, by be/bi (1)
for rent ta ojora (23)
for sale ta biyuu (21)
forbidden to abaau (14)
foreigner kawaaja (*pl* kawajaat) (8)
forest, countryside gaba (29)
form wornii (18)
forty arbeyiin (14)
four arba (1)
four hundred orbomiiya (15)
fourteen arbataasher (14)
France Faraansa (17)
free, empty fadi (6)
French Faraansi (10)
Friday yom juma (16)
fridge talaaja (22)
fried muhaamur (6)
friend sabii (14)
frog gony/gowany (*pl* gowanyaat) (34)
from min (3)
fruit fawaaki (2)
fruit juice asiir (32)
fruit trees fawaaki (12)
future, indefinite bi *(aux)* (7)

G

game, match mubaraa (16)
garden jineena (*pl* jinenaat) (12)
gas jaz (22)
gasoline, petrol benziin (30)
gate, door bab (*pl* babaat) (4)
Germany Almaania (18)
get down nenzil/nezil (14)
get on, ride, climb up arkabu (4)
get to be, become biga (13); tala (34)
get up, wake up gum (27)
giraffe zaraaf (14)

girl biniiya (*pl* biniyaat/banaat) (10)
give, hand, bring jibu (1)
give, take, lend to wadii/wodii (19)
give birth weledu/welidu (7)
glass cup kubaaya (*pl* kubayaat) (5)
go/went ruwa/rowa; masi/mashi (2)
go bamshi (32)
go out, go over, exceed tala (9)
goal gon (16)
goat ganamooya (*pl* ganamoyaat) (26)
God Alaa(h) (25)
good, well, okay kweis(a)/kwesii (*pl* kweisiin) (1)
good heavens! ya salaam (8)
goodbye maasalaam taki/takum (1)
goods, cargo budaa (20)
government hukuuma (31)
grain, millet, sorghum dura (1)
grandfather jidi (13)
grandmother abuuba (13)
greens koroofo (2); kudru (*pl* kudruwaat) (2)
ground, earth wataa (34)
groundnuts ful (2)
grow, plant zarau (ed.) (21)
guest, visitor defaan (*pl* defanaat) (3); def (*pl* diyuuf) (ed.) (5)
guilty galtaan (26)

H

hair shaar/shahar (22)
half nus (2)
half (of a football game) shot (16)
half and half nus nus (10)
hand *(n)*; handle; arm ida (*pl* ideen (4)
hand *(v)*; give; bring jibu (1)
happen hasil (26)
happy moksuut (32)
hard, difficult sab (11)
hard, dried up gowi (21)
have indu/andu (10)

have, possess fi (1)
have to, must lazim (9)
hawk, shrike guraab (*pl*
     gurabaat) (34)
he/him, she/her, it huwo/huwa (1)
head ras (28)
health, body gisim (13)
hear, listen, obey asumu/asma(u)
     (2)
heavy, thick tegiil (11)
hello salaam; salaam taki *(sg),*
     salaam takum *(pl);* salamaat
     (sg), salamaatkum *(pl)* (1)
help *(v)* saaidu (8)
helpless, poor miskiin (33)
helplessness miskiin (34)
her/she, him/he, it huwo/huwa (1)
here is yauu de (11)
her(s), of her to(u)/bitoo(u) (1)
hey yala (5)
hide dusu (34)
hill, mountain jebel (12)
him/he, her/she, it huwo/huwa (1)
Hindu Hindi (10)
his, of him to(u)/bitoo(u) (1)
history tariik (31)
hit, knock, clap dugu (4)
hold, take amsiku (26)
hole hofra (34)
holiday, days off bataala (32)
holiday, feast id (32)
hot sukun (15)
hour, watch sa (*pl* sa-aat) (4)
house, home bet (*pl* biyuut) (3)
house, inside place juwa (*pl*
     juwaat) (15)
house worker kadaam (*pl*
     kadamaat/kadamiin) (14)
how kef (4)
how much/many kam (1)
hundred miya (14)
hungry ja-aan/jaan (I)
hunt, shoot durubu (14)

I

I/me ana (1)
I have indi (ed.) (13)
ice telij (22)
if, when kan (5)
if you will; please kan ita asma/
     kan ta asma (10)
in fi
in a little while bad(i) shweya (9)
in it fogo
in order to ashaan (8)
indefinite, future bi *(aux)* (7)
injure awagu (28)
inside juwa (12)
inside place, house juwa (*pl*
     juwaat) (23)
intelligent, clever shatir (7)
iron, ironing mokwa (15)
is it true that...? seii (5)
island jeziira (*pl* jeziraat) (12)
isn't it good? musu/muze kweis (11)
isn't that so? muze (de)? (6)
it, he/him, she/her huwo/huwa (1)
its, of it to(u)/bitoo(u) (1)
ivory aj (14)

J

jalabiya jalabiiya (11)
Jesus Yesuua (32)
juice made of fruit asiir (32)
just, now hasi de (4)
just, only sakit (31)

K

kabob kabaab (5)
keeper, owner sid (1)
kerosine, paraffin jaz abiyad (22)
key muftaa (*pl* muftahaat) (9)
kill katalu (34)
kilo kilo (2)
kind, shape shikil (21)
kind of abu (9)
kitchen motbak/juwa motbak (15)

knife sikiin (22)
knock, clap, hit dugu (4)
know arifu/arufu (1)
know how, be able to, can bagder (10)

L

language rotaan (Intro)
large, big kebiir (9)
large envelope, parcel zerif al kebiir (9)
last, previous al fat (15)
lastly nihaaya (18)
late *(adj)* muta-akir (27); *see also* be late
late afternoon, evening ashiiya (27)
lazy kaslaan (22)
leafy green vegetable kudru/kudra (*pl* kudruwaat) (11)
learn alimu (3)
leather, skin jilid (19)
leave sibu (19)
left (not right), north shamaal (5)
leg, foot kureen (28)
lemon(s), lemonade lemuun (2)
lemonade moya lemuun (2)
lend to; give; take wadii/wodii (19)
less, minus ila (6)
lesson deris (*pl* derisiaat) (1)
let kelii (9)
letter, answer jawaab (*pl* jawabaat) (9)
license ruksa/roksa (14)
lift, raise arfau (34)
light (weight) kafiif (11)
like, as ze (21)
like, love hebu (32)
lime(s) lemuun (12)
line, queue, section safa (*pl* safaat) (9)
lining gumaash fi juwa (19)
listen, hear, obey asumu/asma(u) (2)

listen please asma ita (9)
little shweya (2)
live, stay geni (4)
liver kibda (*pl* kibdaat) (6)
living room (oda) juluus (7)
long, tall tawiil (11)
long ones, tall ones tuwaliin (11)
long time ago bedri (28); zamaan (34)
look, see ainu (3); shuf(u) (3)
look for fetishu (29)
Lord Rabuuna (8)
lorry, truck lori (4)
lose/lost woduru (9)
love, like hebu (32)
luggage afashaat (24)
lunch/dinner (early afternoon) gada (15)

M

machine makana (*pl* makanaat) (11)
made *(pass)* amuluu (3)
made, ready jahiz (11)
magazine jeriida (22)
maize, corn isheriif (1)
make, do amulu/amalu (3)
malaria malaaria (28)
mama, mommy mama (7)
man rajil (*pl* rujaliin) (2)
mango manga (*pl* mangaat) (2)
many/much ketiir (2)
market suk (*pl* sukaat) (2)
married *(pass)* zowijuu (10)
marry zowiju (10)
match, game mubaraa (16)
material, cloth, clothes gumaash (*pl* gumashaat) (11)
matter, case kalaam (26)
mattress, bed martaba (22)
may kelii (8)
me/I ana (1)
meal akil (*pl* akilaat) (6)
meaning mana (10)

meat laam/laham (1)
Mecca Maka (33)
mechanic makaniiki (8)
medicine dawa (*pl* dawaat) (26)
meet limu (8); ligoo (14)
memorize zekiru (10)
men rujaliin (*sg* rajil) (2)
menu waraga ta akilaat (6)
Messiah, Christ Mesiihi (32)
milk leben (Intro)
millet, sorghum, grain dura (1)
million milyoon (15)
mine, my, of me bitaai (2)
ministry wizaara (20)
minus, less ila (6)
minute degiiga (*pl* degaayg) (9)
mommy, mama mama (7)
Monday yom itniini (15)
money guruush (1)
monkey girid (*pl* guruud) (14)
month saar/shahar (*pl* shuhuur) (3)
more ziada (1)
morning sabaa (10)
most kalis (32)
mother uma (*pl* umahaat) (7)
mother's brother (uncle) kal (13)
mother's sister (aunt) kalti (13)
motorcycle bodaboda (5)
mountain, hill jebel (12)
mourn, cry kori/kore (25)
mourning bika (25)
movie, film filim (31)
much/many ketiir (2)
Muslim *(n)* Muslim (*pl* Muslimiin) (32)
must, have to lazim (9)
my, mine, of me tai/bitaai (2)
my father abuuy (25)

N

name isim (17)
nationality jinis (18)

nations umam (8); *see* United Nations
near (to) geriib (ma) (4)
need, want deru (1); azu/aju/auju (1) (ed. *pl* deriin) (1)
neighbor jeraan (*pl* jeranaat) (8)
never mind, sorry mata fekiru (4); maleesh (5)
new jediid (11)
news kabar (*pl* akbar) (13)
next, coming al jay (16)
night bileel (23)
nine tisa (2)
nine hundred tusomiiya (15)
nineteen tisataasher (19)
ninety tiseyiin (14)
no la' (1)
nomadic travel rahalu (29)
north, left shamaal (5)
not ma (1); musu/muze (11)
not good ma kweis (11)
not yet, still lisa (3)
notebook nota (18)
now, just hasi de (4)
number nimira (*pl* nimiraat) (1)

O

obey, hear, listen asumu/asma(u) (2)
occasion, time wokit (8)
occupation waziifa (18)
of, belong to ta/bitaa (2)
of course, certainly lazim (9)
of him, his; of her, hers; of it, its to(u)/bitoo(u) (1)
of me, my, mine tai/bitaai (2)
of them, their(s) tomon/bitoomon (2)
of us, our(s) taniina/bitaniina (2)
of you, your(s) *(pl)* takum/bitaakum (1)
of you, your(s) *(sg)* taki/ bitaaki (1)

office maktab (*pl* maktabaat)
(5)
official *(n)* afeendi (*pl*
afeendiyaat) (15)
official, office worker,
employee muwaazif (8)
oil zet (1)
okay teb (9)
okay, finished kalaas (1)
okay, good, well kweis(a)/kwesii
(*pl* kweisiin) (1)
old (person) ajuus (28)
old (thing) gediim (11)
old times gediim (29)
on it fogo (15)
on one's own baraau (17)
once, one time, one turn dor
wahid (14)
one wahid/waid (9)
one fourth rubu (6)
one hundred miya (14)
one million milyoon (15)
one quarter rubu (6)
one third tilit (6)
one thousand alf (15)
one time, one turn, once dor
wahid (14)
onion basal (*pl* basalaat) (29)
onion(s) basal (29)
only bes (8)
only, just sakit (31)
open fata(u) (4)
or wala (3); au (32)
orange *(n)* bordokaal (12)
order, request talab (Intro)
organization munaazama (18)
other tani (1)
others taniin (1)
our, of us taniina (2)
outing rihla (14); ziyaara (12)
outside bara (4)
over gabulu (11)
owner, keeper sid (1)

P

pain waja (13)
pants, trousers bantoloon (*pl*
bantolonaat) (11)
paper *(n)* waraga (*pl* waragaat) (6)
paraffin, kerosine jaz abiyad (22)
parcel, large envelope zerif al
kebiir (9)
parlor, living room (oda) juluus (7)
party hafla (*pl* haflaat) (17)
passport pasport (18)
pastor, priest abuuna (24)
pay dafau (9)
peace (greeting) salaam (1)
peace to you (greeting) salaam
taki *(sg);* salaam takum *(pl)*
peanuts, groundnuts ful (2)
peck, beat dugu (34), togu (34)
pen, pencilgalam (*pl* galamaat)
(7)
people nas *(sg* zol) (12)
period of time muda (3); zaman
(13); wokit (13)
person zol (*pl* nas) (3)
petrol, gasoline benziin (30)
phone *(n)* telefoon (20)
phone *(v);* ring (a bell) durubu/
udrubu (20)
picture sura (*pl* suraat) (11)
pile kom (2)
pilgrimage to Mecca hej (33)
pink bembi (21)
place mahaal (*pl* mahalaat)/maal
(*pl* malaat) (2)
plant *(n);* flower zuhuur (21)
plant *(v);* grow zarau (21)
play, dance alabu (7)
player lahib (16)
please (invitation) fadal (3)
please, if you will kan ita asma/
kan ta asma (10)
poor, helpless, helplessness
miskiin (33)

possess; have fi (1)
possible mumkin (9)
post busta (9)
post office maktab busta (9)
potato(es) bataatis (2)
pound (SSP=South Sudanese
    Pound) jinee (1)
pound, beat durubu/udrubu (20)
pour kubu (21)
pray seli (24)
prayer salaa (*pl* salawaat) (24)
pretty, beautiful jemiil (12)
pretty, sweet helu (12)
previous, last al fat (15)
price (*n*) taman (19)
priest, pastor abuuna (24)
problem, trouble mushkila (*pl*
    mashaakil) (24)
progressive ge/gi (4)
project moshruu' (20)
pull juru (34)
pupil, student tilmiis (Intro)
put kutu (22)
put into, cause to enter dakalu/
    dakulu (9)
put on, wear libisu (24)

Q
quarter rubu (6)
question (*n*) asila (*pl* asilaat) (2)
question (*v*) asala (14)
queue, line, sectionsafa (*pl*
    safaat) (9)

R
radio radio (10)
rain matar (29)
rainy season kariif (29)
raise, lift arfau (34)
Ramadan Ramadaan (33)
read agra (18)
ready, made jahiz (11)
reason sabab (31)

recent geriib (ma) (8)
red amer (21)
redivision kokoora (Intro)
reduce, discount (*v*) nagisu (2)
refrigerator talaaja (22) talaaja (22)
register sejilu (9)
remainder bagi (24)
rent (*n*) ojora (23)
rent (*v*) ajoru (23)
repair sala(u) (5)
reply, answer (*v*) jawabu (10)
request, order talab (Intro)
reservation hejiz (27)
restaurant kuluub (6)
return rija (4)
review muraaja (10)
rice ruz (1)
ride, get on, climb up arkabu (4)
right (not left) yamiin (5)
right, correct sah (10)
ring (a bell); phone (*v*) durubu/
    udrubu (20)
river, sea baar/bahar (7)
river, stream, creek bed kor (*pl*
    koraat) (29)
road, way teriig (5)
room oda (*pl* odaat) (3)
roundabout siniiya (5)
ruined karabu (5); kasuru (15)
run jere (34)

S
sacrifice (*v*) dabaau (26)
safe, well (*adj*) ker (30)
salad salata (6)
salary mohiiya (*pl* mowaahi) (31)
salt mile (1)
same wahid/waid (9)
Saturday (yom) sebit (16)
sauce, stew mulaa(h) (22)
say, tell kelimu (7)
school medreesa/medereesa (3)
scissors magaas (22)

score sejilu (16)
sea, river baar/bahar (7)
secretary sikirteer (8)
section, line, queuesafa (*pl* safaat) (9)
self yauu (11)
sell, buy biyuu (11)
send rasulu (9)
seven saba (2)
seven hundred subumiiya (15)
seventeen sabataasher (17)
seventy sebeyiin (14)
sew keitu (11)
sewing kayaata (11)
sewing machine makana (*pl* makanaat) (11)
shape, kind shikil (21)
sharp siniin (22)
she/her, he/him, it huwo/huwa (1)
sheep kuruuf (*pl* kurufaat) (26)
shirt gemiis (*pl* gemissiyaat) (11)
shoot, hunt durubu (14)
shop, store dukaan (*pl* dukanaat) (1)
short guseer (12)
show awaaru (31); worii (23)
shrike, hawk guraab (*pl* gurabaat) (34)
shrub, tree shejara (*pl* shejaraat) (21)
shut, close *(v)* gofulu/gofolu (4)
sick ayaan (4)
sick ones ayaniin (4)
significant event marker gum (35)
sir sabi (6)
sister okot/ukut (*pl* ikwaat) (13)
sisters and/or brothers akwaana (4)
sit (down), stay, live geni (3)
six sita (2)
six hundred sutumiiya (15)
sixteen sitaasher (16)
sixty sitiin (14)

skin, leather jilid (19)
skinny, thin jogoot (12)
slaughter dabaau (26)
sleep num (10)
small sukeer (11)
soap sabuun (1)
soft leyin (22)
some taniin (32)
son, boy, child weled/welid/ woled (*pl* awlaad) (2)
sorghum, millet, grain dura (1)
sorry, never mind maleesh (5)
so-so kida u kida (16)
soup shurba (6)
south januub (30)
South Sudan Januub Sudaan (5)
    South Sudanese (n) Januub Sudaani (*pl* Januub Sudaniin) (5)
South Sudanese Pound (SSP) jinee (1)
specialist, expert zol indu fikra (18)
specifically yauu (6)
spoon malaga (22)
stadium dar riyaada (16)
stamp *(n)* tabe (*pl* tawaabe) (9)
stamp, stomp *(trans)* dusu (34)
stand, stop wogufu/wagif(u) (4)
stay, live geni (4)
stew, sauce mulaa(h) (22)
still, not yet lisa (3)
stomp, stamp *(trans)* dusu (34)
stop, stand wogufu/wagif(u) (4)
store, shop dukaan (*pl* dukanaat) (1)
storm, wind habuub (Intro)
story gisa (34)
straight (ahead) tawaali (Intro)
straight (line) adiil (5)
stream, river, creek bed kor (*pl* koraat) (29)
street sharia (8)
student taliba (*pl* talibaat) (10); tilmiis (Intro)

studio istiidiu (24)
study derisu/deresu (3)
sugar sukar (1)
summer, dry season sef (29)
Sunday yom lahad (16)
supervisor masuul (31)
supper asha (3)
surface mail beriid al adi (9)
surrounding, around hawe (17)
sweet, pretty helu (12)
sweets, candy alaawa (*pl* alawaat) (33)
swell woromu (28)
swelling woroma (28)
sympathy kafaara (13)

T

table terebeeza (*pl* terebezaat) (5)
take (away) shilu (14)
take, give, lend to wadii/wodii (19)
take, hold amsiku (26)
take off gum (34)
take pictures sowru (12)
talk, dialogue *(n)* kalaam (26)
tall, long tawiil (11)
tall ones, long ones tuwaliin (11)
taste jeribu (22)
taxi teksi (Intro)
tea shay (1)
teach derisu/deresu (8)
teacher mudeeris (*pl* muderisiin/ muderisiaat) (5)
telephone *(n)* telefoon (20)
telephone *(v)* udrubu/ durubu (20)
television tilivizyoon (31)
tell, say kelimu (7)
ten ashara (2)
thank you shukran/sukuran (1)
that dak (3)
that means yani (6)
the next, the coming al jay (16)
their(s), of them tomon/bitoomon (2)

them/they humon (1)
then badiin/badeen (5)
there hinaak (12)
there is/are; exist fi (1)
these del (10)
they/them humon (1)
they have indum (ed.) (13)
thick, heavy tegiil (11)
thin, skinny jogoot (12)
thing haja (*pl* hajaat) (1)
think fekiru (4)
third tilit (6)
thirsty atshaan (34)
thirteen talataasher (13)
thirty teletiin (14)
this de (1)
this one here yauu de (11)
this very *(emphasis)* zatu (8)
thousand alf (15)
three talaata/telaata (2)
Thursday yom kamiis (16)
ticket taskar(a) (27)
time, occasion wokit (8)
time, turn dor (14)
tired tabaan (34)
to fi (2); le (1)
to me lei; le ana (17)
today aleela/naar de (5)
toilet mustraa (23); bakaan
told me to ni-/no- (22)
tomorrow bukra (7)
too much/many ketiir (2)
travel safiru (4)
traveling safar (30)
tree, shrub shejara (*pl* shejaraat) (21)
trees for fruit fawaaki (12)
trial (at court) gediiya (26)
tribe gabiila (29)
trouble, problem mushkila (*pl* mashaakil) (24)
trousers, pants bantoloon (*pl* bantolonaat) (11)
truck, lorry lori (4)

trunk of an elephant ida (34)
Tuesday yom talataa; yom
   salasaa (16)
turn, circle around lifu (24)
turn, time dor (14)
turn over gilibu (30)
tusk sunuun (*pl* sununaat) (14)
TV tilivizyoon (31)
twelve itnaasher (6)
twenty ishriin (8)
twice itiniin dor (14)
two itiniin/itniin (1)
two days yomeen (32)
two hundred miteen (15)
type *(v)* tabau (20)

U

uncle (father's brother) akuu
   abuu (13)
uncle (mother's brother) kal (13)
under, down, below teet/tehet (7)
understand afamu (10); alimu (3)
united muteeheda (8)
United Nations Umam al
   Muteeheda (8)
university jama (5)
until le hadi/li hadi (5); naman (34)
up, above fog (7)
us/we aniina (1)

V

very shediid (6); kalis (2)
village, country beled (8)
visit, outing ziyaara (12)
visitor, guest defaan (*pl* defanaat)
   (3); def (*pl* diyuuf) (ed.) (5)
vocative ya (2)

W

wait a minute degiiga (9)
waiter jarasoon (*pl* jarasonaat) (6)
wake up, get up gum (34)
walk *(n)* dowriiya (12)

walk *(v* dowru (12)
want, needderu (1); azu/aju/auzu/
   auju (1) (ed. *pl* deriin) (1)
warm up sakanu (16)
was kan (5)
was brought jibuu (8)
wash kasulu (7)
watch, hour sa (*pl* sa-aat) (4)
water moya (3)
water tap masuura (23)
way, road teriig (5)
we/us aniina (1)
we have indana (ed.) (13)
wear, put on libisu (24)
weather jo
wedding iris (24)
Wednesday yom arbaa (16)
week usbuu (7)
weight wazin (9)
welcome (greeting) ahlen (1); *see
   also* you're welcome
well *(n)* bir (*pl* biraat) (29)
well, good, okay kweis(a)/kwesii
   (*pl* kweisiin) (1)
well, safe *(adj)* ker (30)
went/go ruwa/rowa; masi/mashi (2)
west garb (Intro)
western garbiiya (18)
what? shunuu (1)
wheat game' (1)
when, if kan (5)
when? miteen (15)
where? wen/wenu (3)
which yatuu (23)
white abiyad (21)
who/which *(relative pro)* al (6)
who/whom? munuu (11)
why? le; le shunuu? (15)
wife, womanmara (*pl* mariaat/
   niswaan) (3)
will be, will become bi kun (13)
wind, storm habuub (Intro)
window shubaak (*pl* shubakaat) (15)

wing (football player) jenaa (16)
with ma/maa (1)
with him/her/it moo; ma huwo (17)
with me mai (17)
with them moom; ma humon (17)
wither, dry up tala gowi (21)
without biduun (24)
woman, wife mara (*pl* mariaat/
    niswaan) (3)
word kelima (*pl* kelimaat) (1)
work *(n)* shokol (8)
work *(v)* ishtaagal (11); takalu (11)
worker shagaal (8); muwaasif (8)
world dunia (32)
wrap robutu (28); lifu (28)
wrapping, bandage rabaat/robaat
    (28)
write/wrote katibu (7)

Y

yard, compound osh (5)
year sena (8)
yellow asfar (21)
yes ai (1)
yesterday umbaari (4)
you *(pl)* itakum (1)
you *(sg)* ita (1)
your(s), of you *(pl)* takum/
    bitaakum (1)
your(s), of you *(sg)* taki/bitaaki (1)
your peace (greeting) salamaat
    (sg); salamaatkum *(pl)*
you're welcome afwan (3); *see also
    welcome (greeting)*

Z

zero sifir (16)

References

Brewster, E. Thomas, and Elizabeth S. 1977. *Language Acquisition Made Practical (LAMP): Field methods for language learners.* Colorado Springs Colo.: Lingua House.

Persson, Andrew, and Janet Persson, with Ahmad Hussein. 1980. *Sudanese Colloquial Arabic for beginners.* High Wycombe, UK: Summer Institute of Linguistics.

Tamis, Rianne, and Janet Persson, eds. 2013. *Sudanese Arabic–English/ English–Sudanese Arabic: A concise dictionary.* Publications in Linguistics 150. Dallas Tex.: SIL International.